Interactive Journal

#UNSTOPPABLE

15 Essential Steps towards Becoming Unstoppable

Lynette Edwards, Author/Life Coach

www.AuthorLynette.com

Published by Priceless Inspirations Publishing

www.pricelessinspirationspublishing.com

ISBN: 978-0692091944

Disclaimer: The purpose of this journal is to empower you on your journey. The actual journey and all decisions made are up to you. The author and publisher are not responsible, nor liable for the outcome of your journey.

"There comes a time when we must release and let go of everything that tears us down, so that we can rebuild ourselves on a strong foundation of what motivates us to become Unstoppable."

— *Lynette Edwards*

This Interactive Journal Belongs to:

_____

Are you reaching your full potential?

Do you have the skills and mindset to make it to the next level?

This interactive journal was created to jumpstart the next level of your life. Regardless of where you currently are in life, now is the perfect moment for you to focus on your future. Think about how reaching your goals and desires can impact your life.

No more excuses. It is time to succeed. It's time to be **UNSTOPPABLE!**

Free Your Mind

How many times have you missed out on opportunities due to trying to multi-task? Let's be honest. It happens more than you realize. You are so busy with the hustle and bustle of everyday life that you simply forget to do everything on your agenda. At times, this can cause you to miss opportunities.

You simply have to free your mind.

Take action steps daily:

Set your daily alarm ten minutes earlier than usual. This will allow you a few minutes each day to get up and think about everything that you have scheduled.

Take a moment and brainstorm. Feel free to write down your daily agenda on paper.

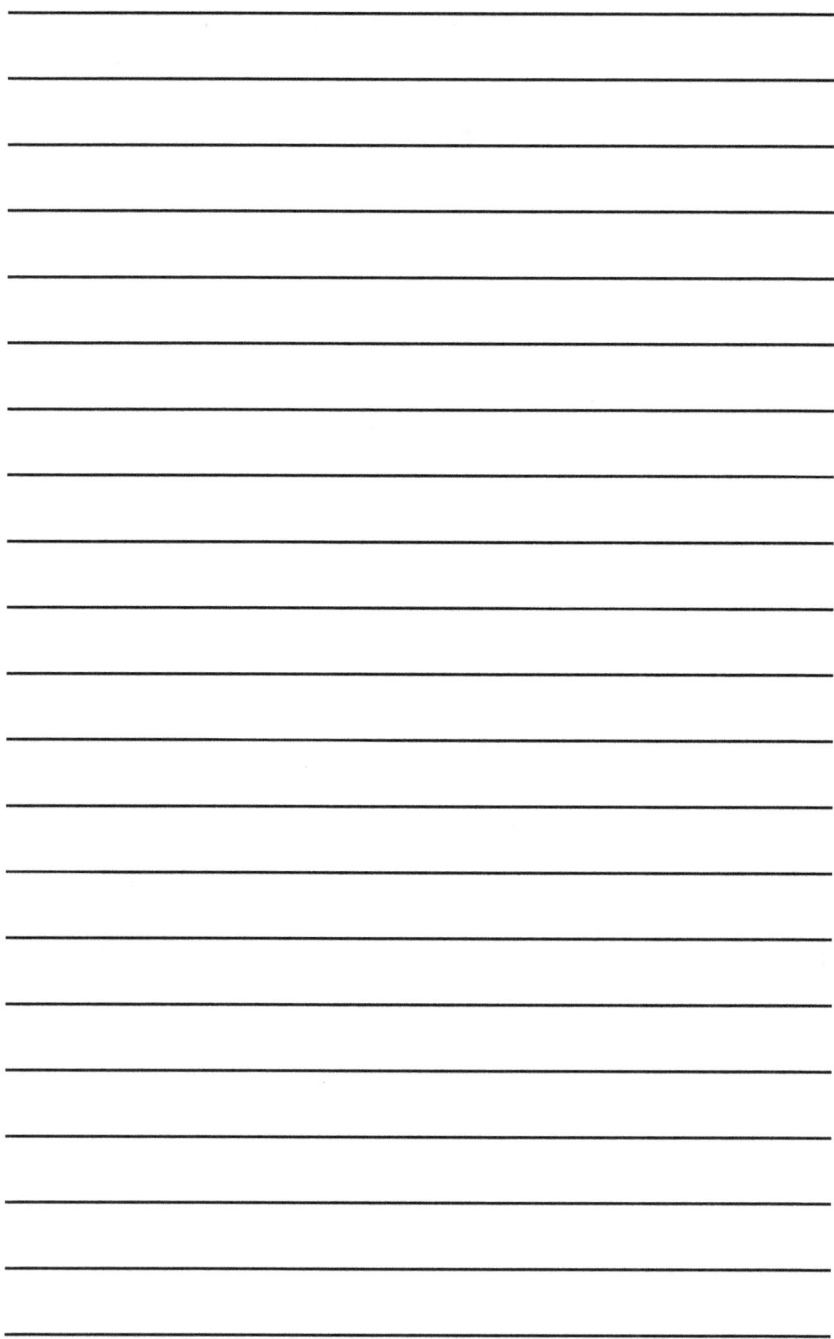

Now that you have a basic understanding of what your day consists of, make a list of your priorities.

_____

_____

_____

_____

_____

_____

_____

_____

_____

_____

_____

_____

_____

_____

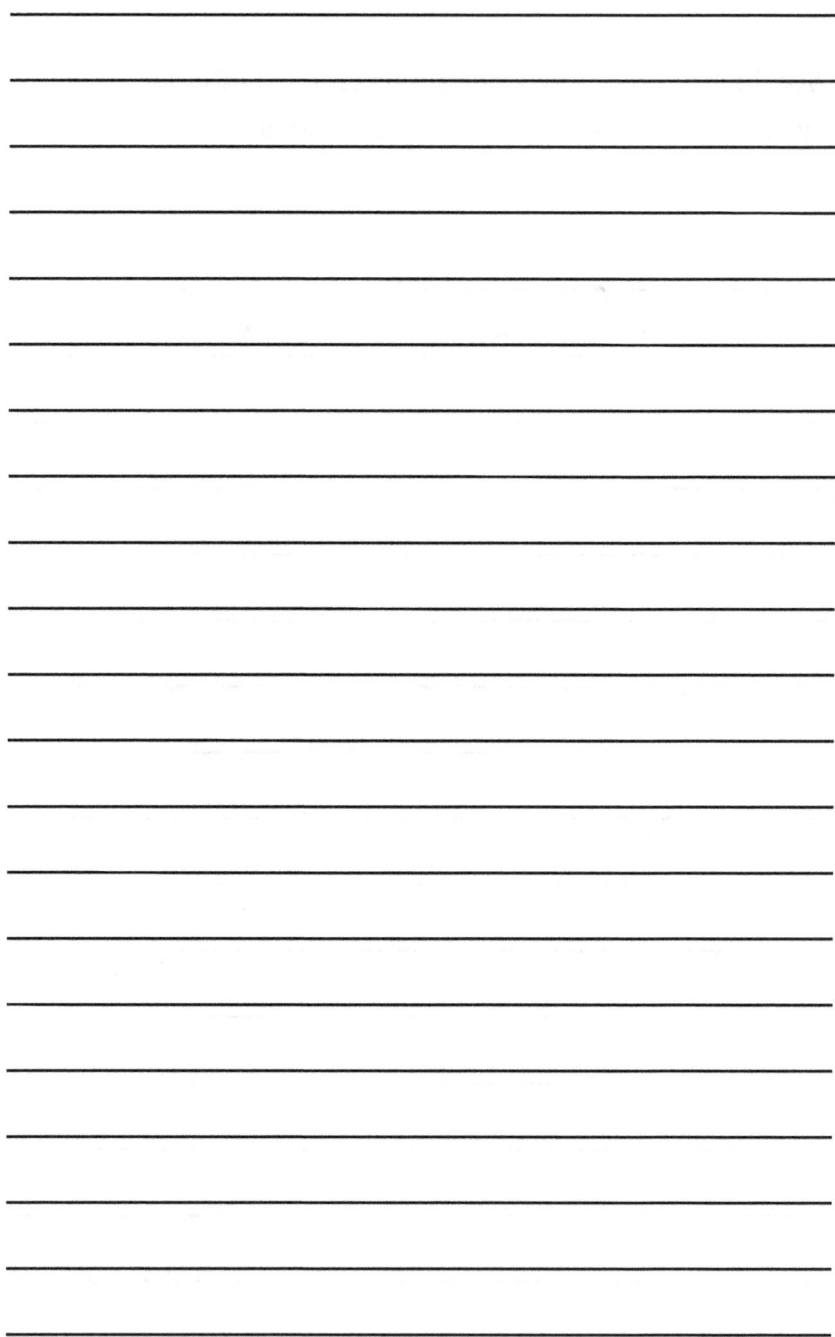

Was there anything that you realized that was on your list that was not a priority? If so, write it down with an expected completion date so that you can get back to it at a later date.

_____

_____

_____

_____

_____

_____

_____

_____

_____

_____

_____

_____

_____

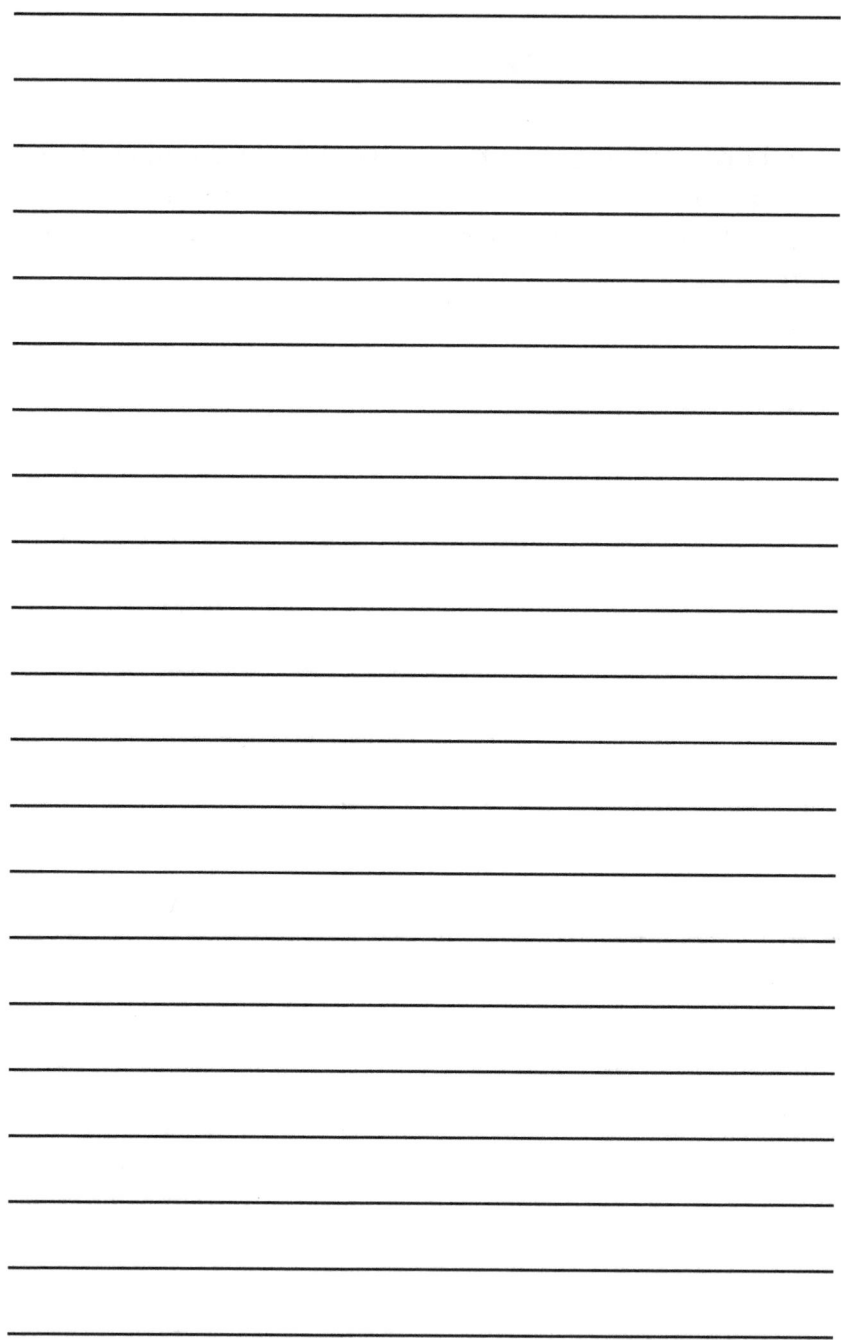

"Release the day dreams of today and focus on the reality of tomorrow."

— *Lynette Edwards*

Now that you have identified your priorities, you need to determine what your steps will be if you become distracted throughout the day. Take a few moments to think about the steps that will help you to refocus after distractions. Write down people, places, things, or ideas that help keep you on track.

_____

_____

_____

_____

_____

_____

_____

_____

_____

_____

_____

_____

_____

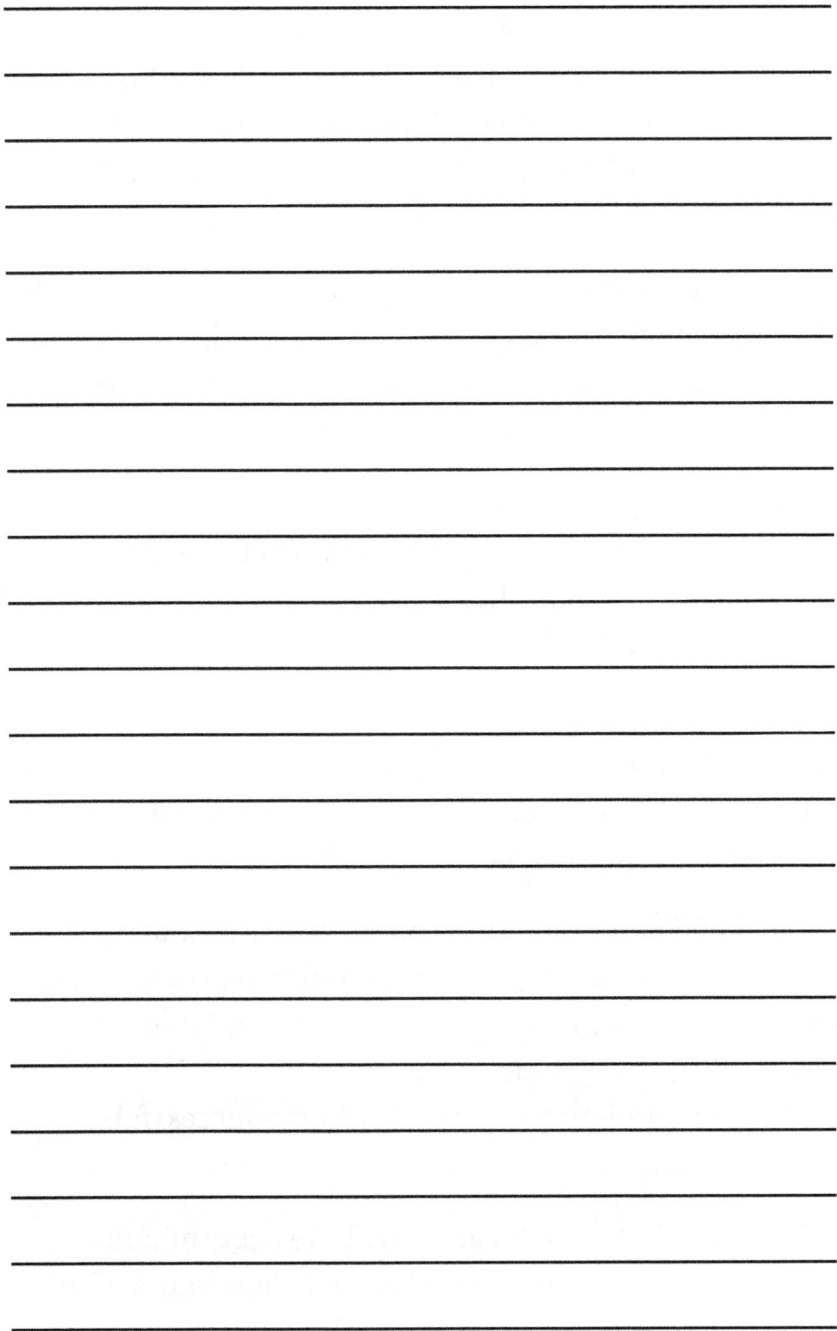

Congratulations!! You have mastered the first essential step in freeing your mind, which is to eliminate distractions and prioritize what matters at the moment. You have also identified ways to help refocus yourself.

Now that you have eliminated all other duties that could have potentially caused you to be distracted, let's focus on your mindset. In order to succeed each day, you have to holistically be free: mind, body, and soul.

Allowing your-self to be free starts from within. You have to mentally regulate your mind. Think positive thoughts. Remember times when you feel more secure in yourself and most of all. . .relax.

Throughout the day, you should remember to take long deep breaths. We all have goals and expectations. But you will not be able to reach your full potential if you are not in a place in your life where your mind is free.

Your mind determines your thoughts. Your thoughts determine your speech, which can ultimately determine your actions. Freeing your mind is an essential part of your success. Many times we neglect the basic necessities in hopes of fulfilling our goals to become successful, forgetting that your mind determines your success.

There are 24 hours in each day. Take a few minutes during that time to sit back, relax, and allow yourself to be free.

I will never in life get to where I am going.

I have been in the business over ten years and I am still not seeing a profit.

What's the point? Maybe it's time to just give up!

When will people realize that I am an amazing person who simply wants to create an above average life for myself?

Let's be real. We are human and we have human emotions. There are times in life when we have been 'Negative Nancy'. Who is 'Negative Nancy'? Simple. She is someone who sees only the negative side of things without realizing that downfalls and hard times are only a part of the natural process.

   Negativity can steam from a plethora of areas, such as past experiences, low self-esteem, no sense of direction, limited guidance, or current unhappiness in multiple areas of life.

_____

Release Negativity

What negative areas are hindering you from reaching your full potential?

_____

_____

_____

_____

_____

_____

_____

_____

_____

_____

_____

_____

_____

_____

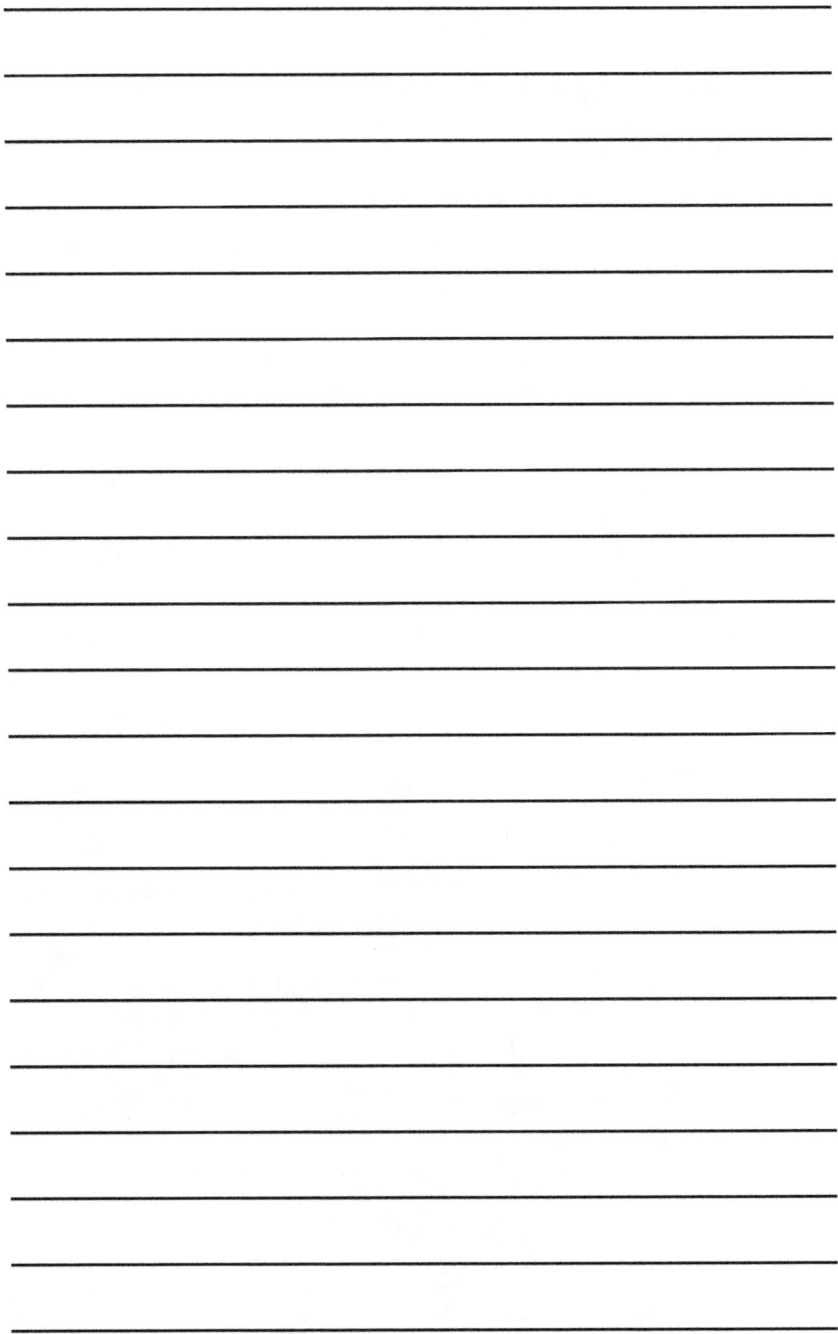

"Don't get hung up on your mess ups, mistakes are inevitable."

- Lynette Edwards

How long have you allowed negativity to hinder you?

_____

_____

_____

_____

_____

_____

_____

_____

_____

_____

_____

_____

_____

_____

_____

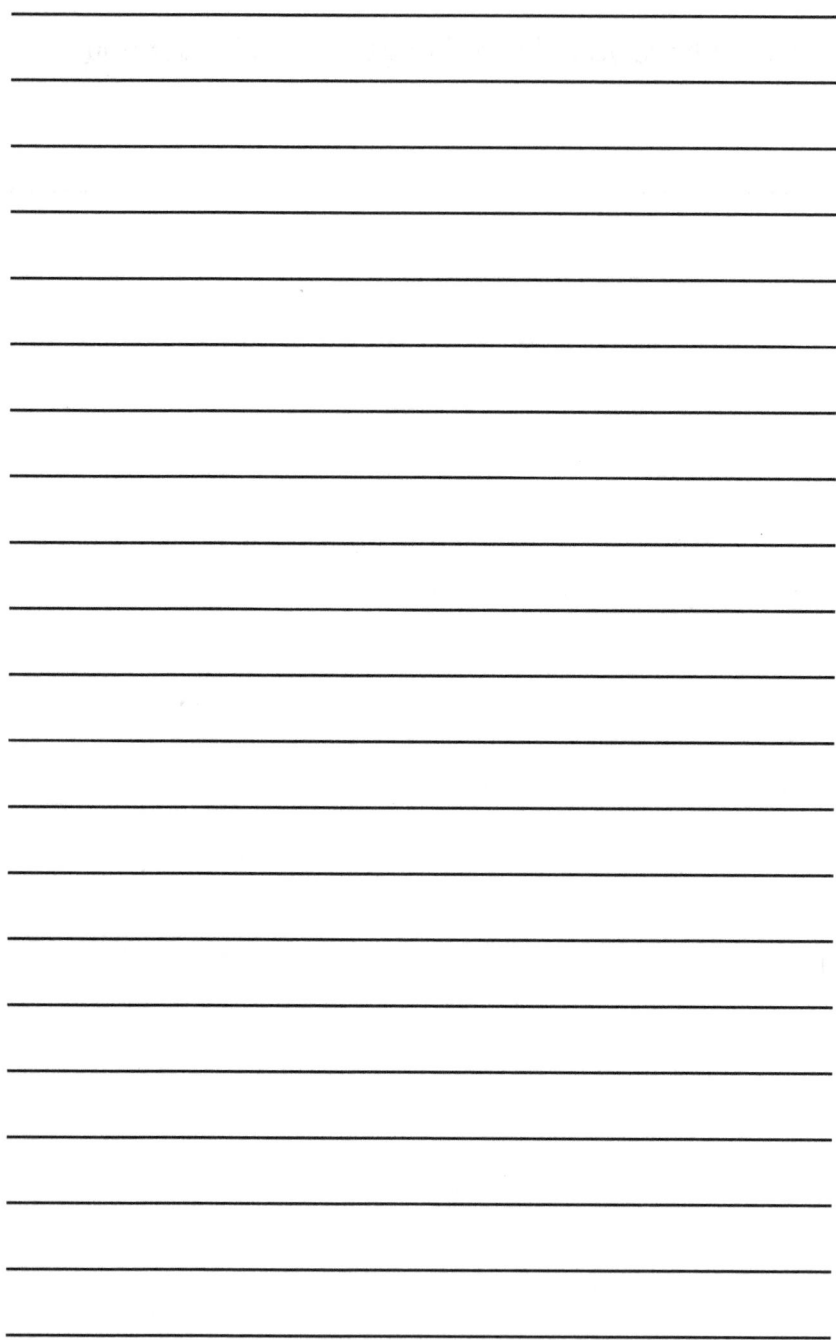

Why have you allowed these areas to hinder you?

_____

_____

_____

_____

_____

_____

_____

_____

_____

_____

_____

_____

_____

_____

_____

_____

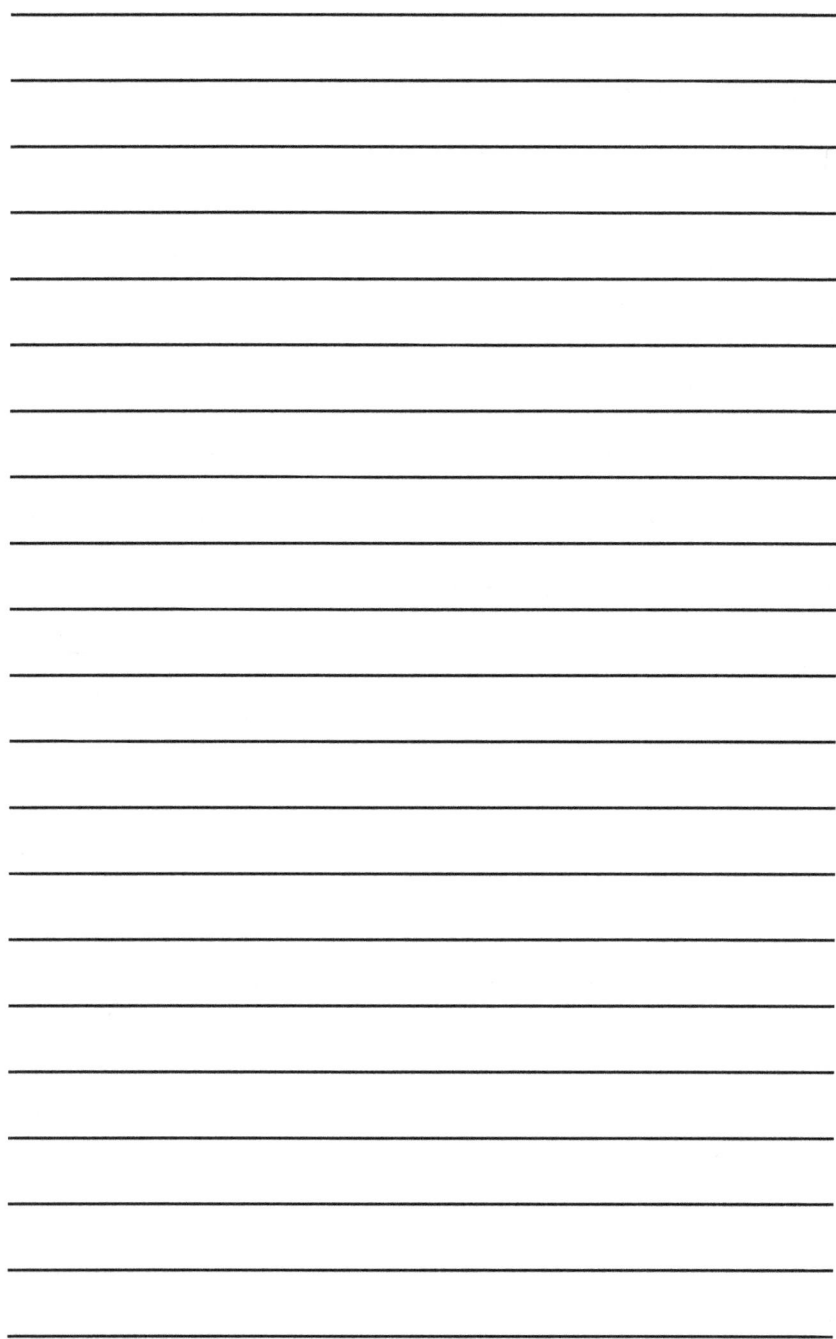

Many people walk in fear. They are scared to release things that hinder them because they are simply fearful of what lies ahead. Holding on to negativity becomes a part of who you are. It hinders you in areas that you may not even realize. Negativity takes from you the one thing that is essential to you being unstoppable. Negativity takes away your inner peace.

It is time to release, let go, and move on. Easier said than done, right? I know. I personally carried negative emotions for many years. I was hurting in areas that I didn't even know existed. But I was determined to release and be free. I had personal goals to reach, books to write, and businesses to run. I needed to release and let go of everything that hindered me.

You have just identified what was hindering you and that means you are now aware of what needs to be released. Will it happen overnight? I highly doubt it. But I can assure you that it will happen if you are honest with yourself and when you allow yourself to heal. Negativity is often more deeply rooted than we talk about. It stems from moments in time when we didn't let go because we were angry. But instead of communicating our feelings, we redirected them somewhere else, which only allowed the negativity to be hidden versus released. No more holding on! No more procrastinating! Let negativity go today!

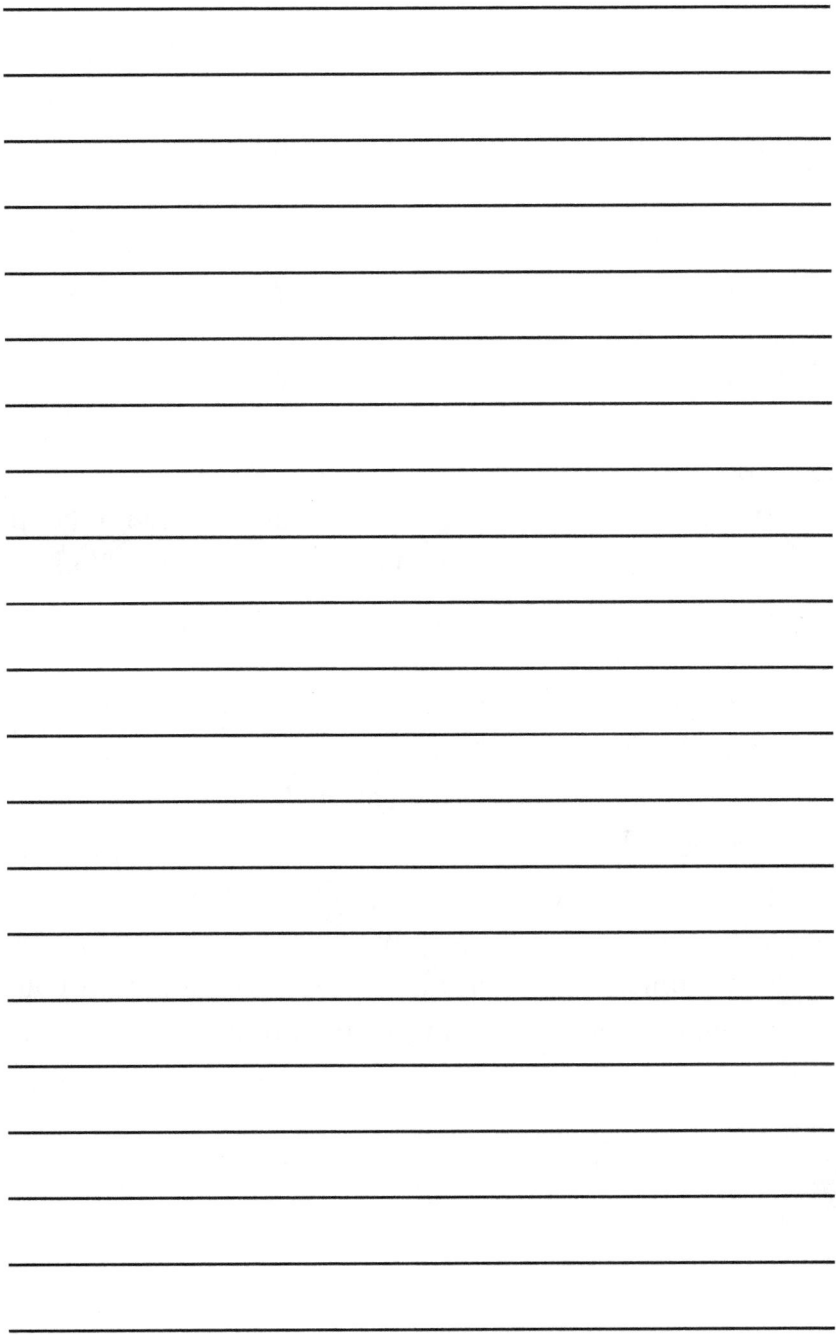

Steps to Release Negativity

1. Identify the source (What is causing negativity in your life?)
2. Identify the effect it is having on your life.
3. Identify your 'calm' place.
4. Identify ways that you can remain calm in times of adversity. You don't want anything to cause you to become negative again.
5. Relax, close your eyes, take a deep breath, and begin to replay in your mind the source of your negativity. You may experience different emotions during this time. It's part of the process. You simply need to keep taking deep breaths and get through this step. You are releasing everything and letting go. It is time. You can't keep holding on. You are destined for greatness. Take your time and release and relax. Repeat this step as many times throughout the day as you need until you have released negative thoughts and anything that may be taking up unnecessary space in your mind. It starts mentally, then (depending on what you are releasing) you may need to openly communicate and verbally release to ensure that you are no longer holding on to what hinders you.

Goal Setting

You have freed your mind and released everything that may have hindered your success. Now it's time to set goals!

Where would you like to be professionally within the next three to six months?

_____

_____

_____

_____

_____

_____

_____

_____

_____

_____

_____

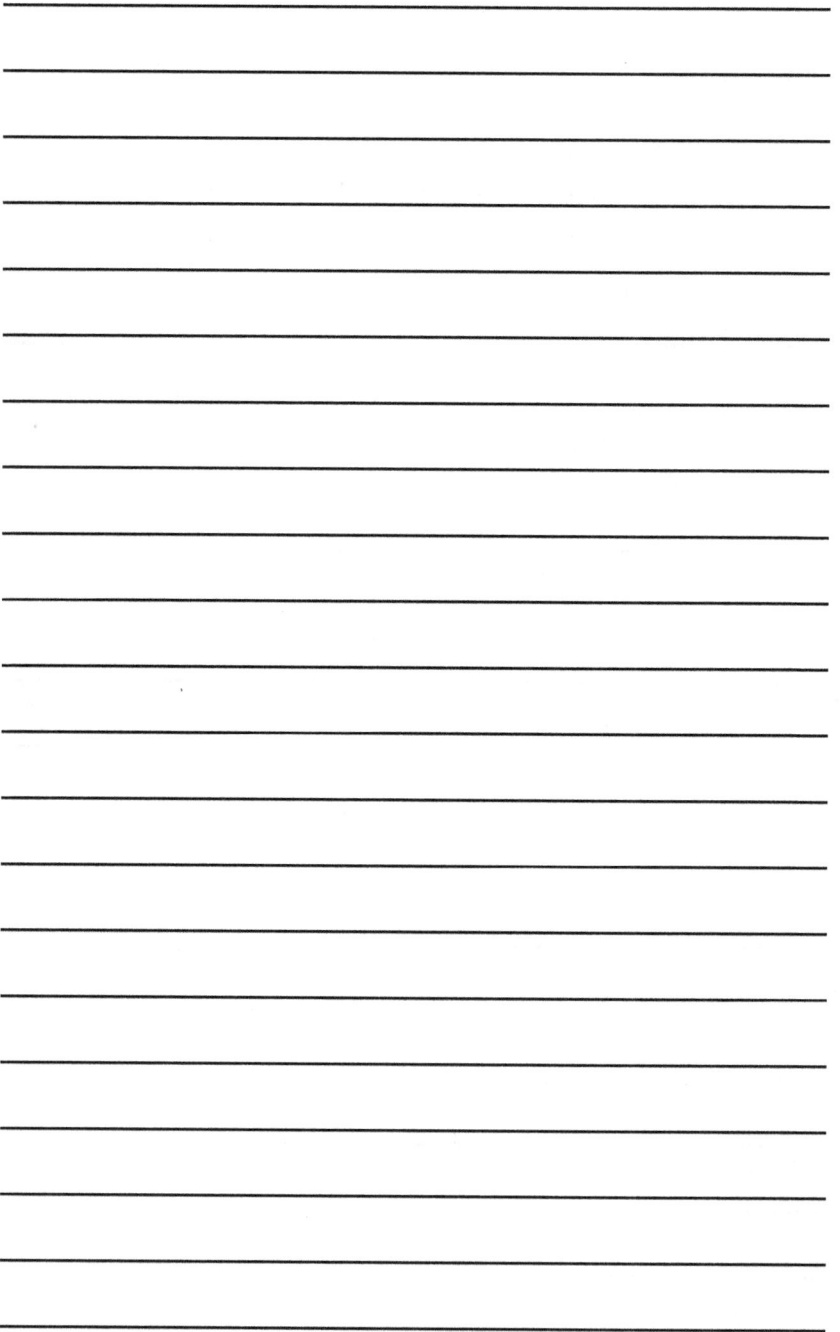

What skills/experience do you currently have that would be beneficial towards reaching your goal(s)?

_____

_____

_____

_____

_____

_____

_____

_____

_____

_____

_____

_____

_____

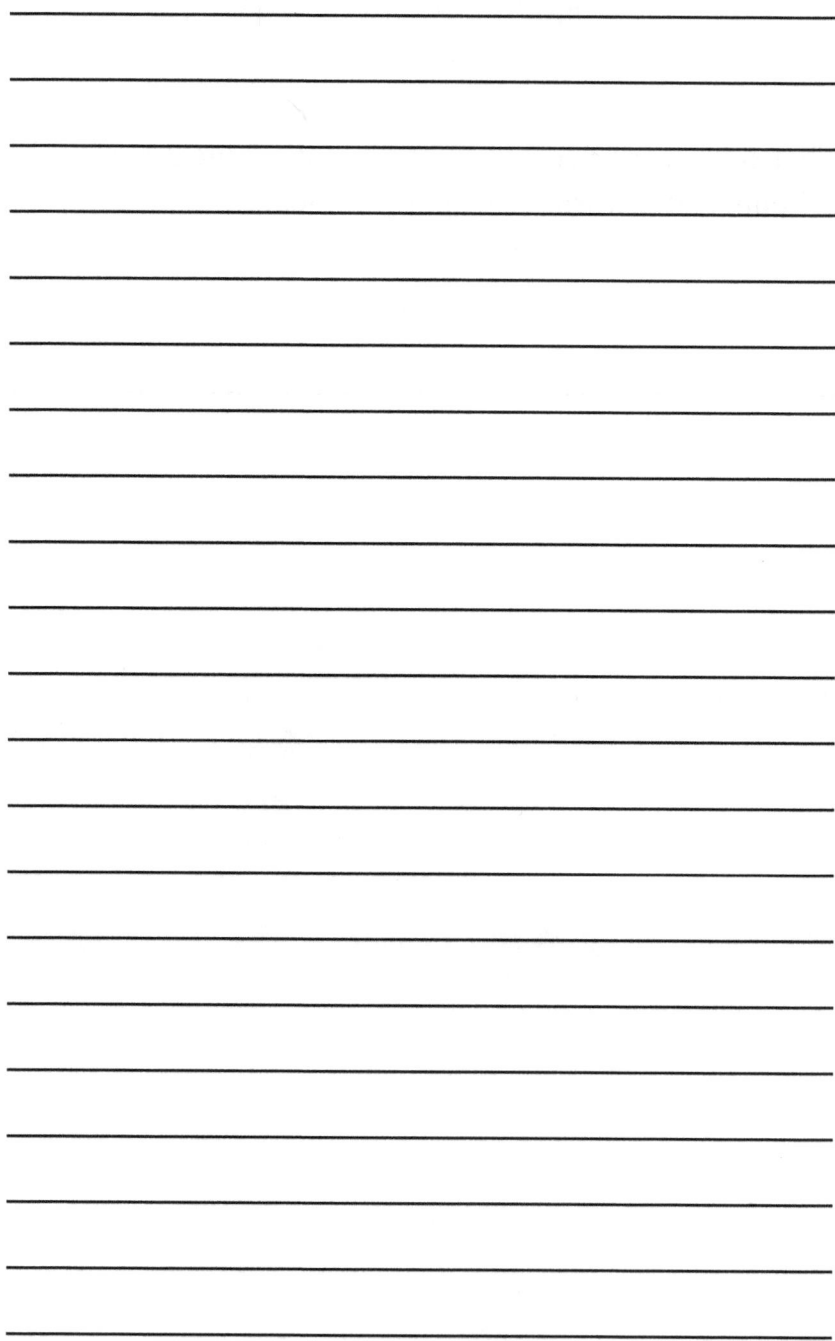

Have you written a business plan? Even if you are not starting your own business, it is essential to have a plan outlined that specifically targets your desires. This will assist you in staying focused on your goals.

_____

_____

_____

_____

_____

_____

_____

_____

_____

_____

_____

_____

_____

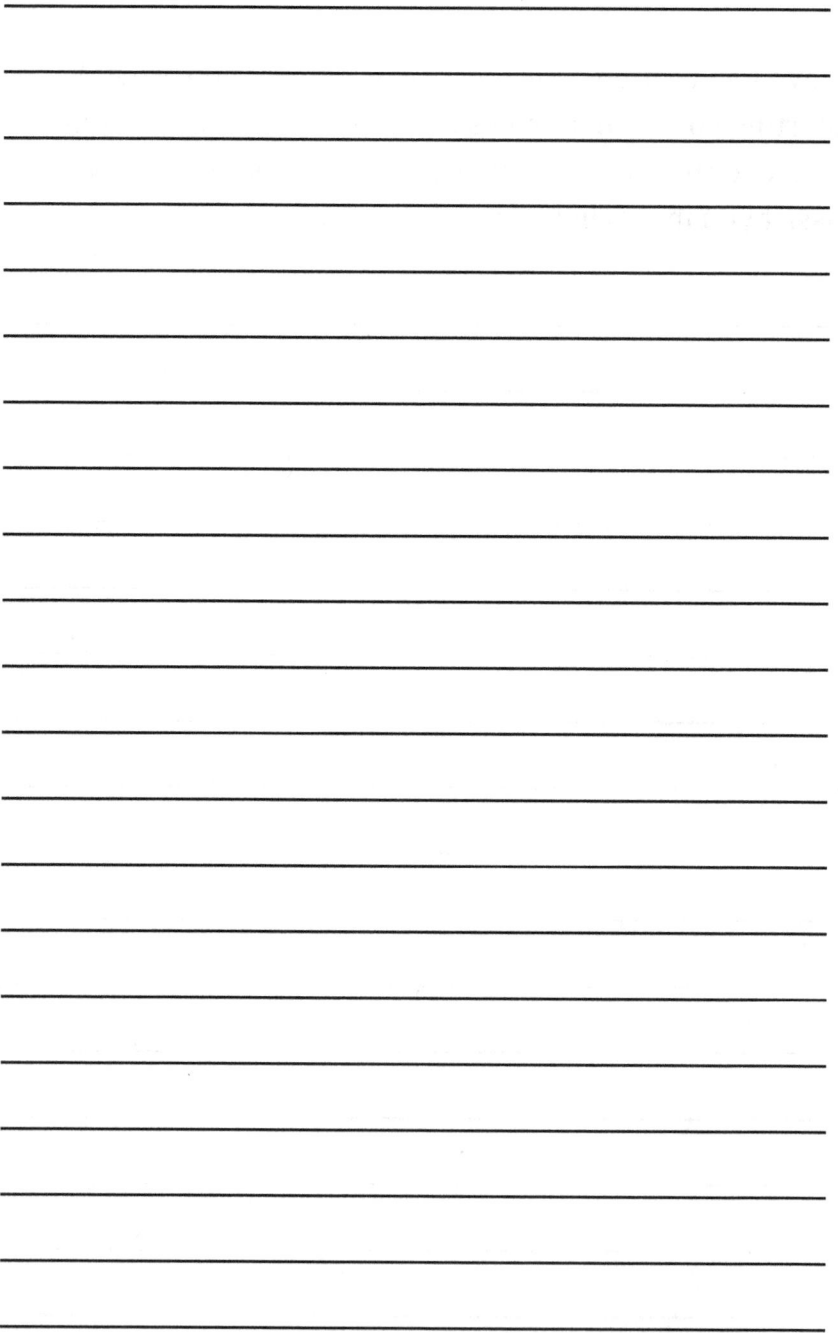

Be mindful when setting goals that every goal is not reachable within three to six months. You should always have obtainable goals so that you are able to reach them. Each goal should be realistic.

For example, let's say that you want to become a published author. Perhaps it's been a desire you've had since you were a child and you are ready to make those childhood dreams come true. Setting a three-month goal of completion is unrealistic. You would want to make this a long-term goal so that you have time to learn every aspect of the business (not to mention the time it takes to actually write the book).

Now let's say that you have already written and edited your book and you are only waiting for the book to be published. If that's the case, then a three-month goal is doable. The average book (once ready for the publishing phase) can be published and ready for print in less than 30 days.

With that said, it is imperative that you set goals that are achievable and obtainable.

What resources will you need to make your goal a reality?

_____

_____

_____

_____

_____

_____

_____

_____

_____

_____

_____

_____

_____

_____

_____

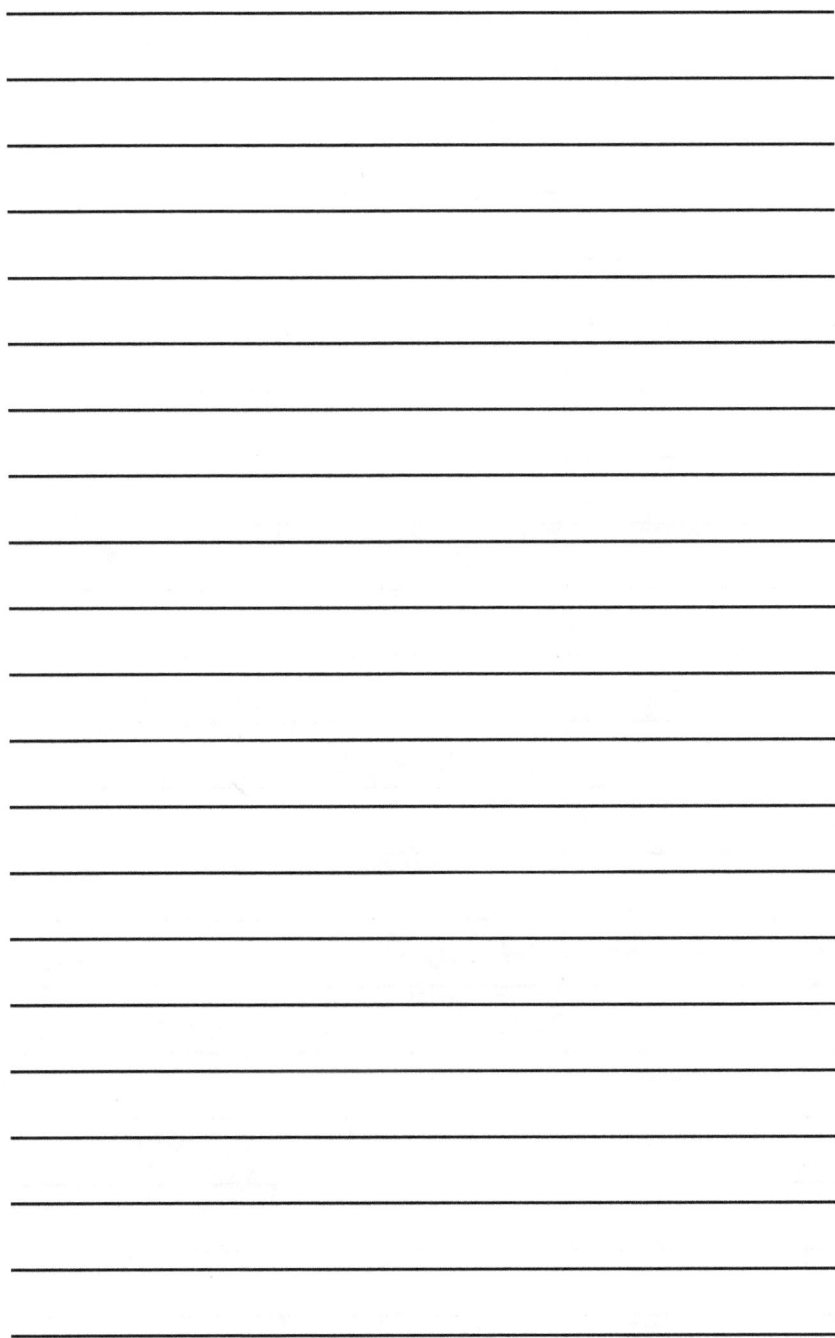

Set specific goals: Be direct when goal setting.

_____

_____

_____

_____

_____

_____

_____

_____

_____

_____

_____

_____

_____

_____

_____

_____

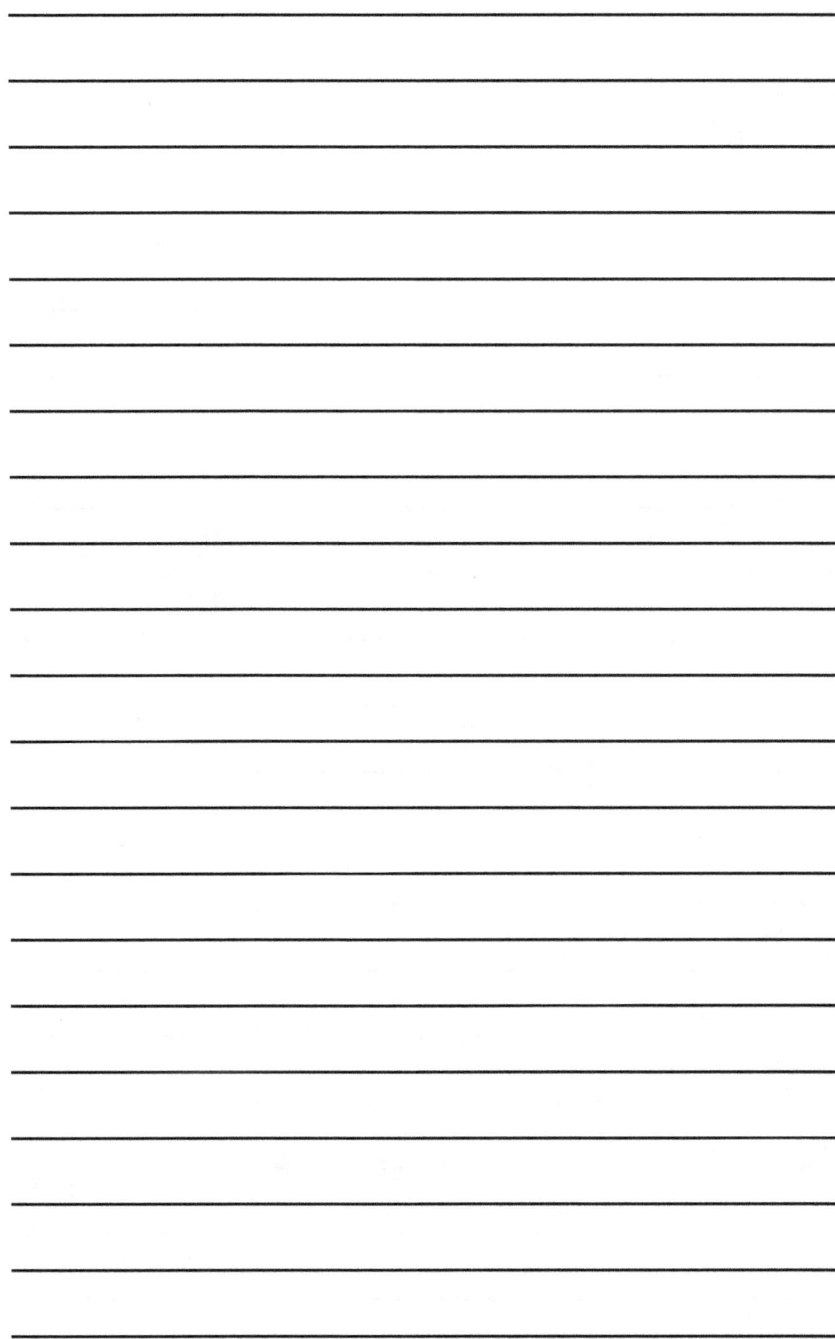

Set a timeline for each goal: When will each goal be reached?

_____

_____

_____

_____

_____

_____

_____

_____

_____

_____

_____

_____

_____

_____

_____

_____

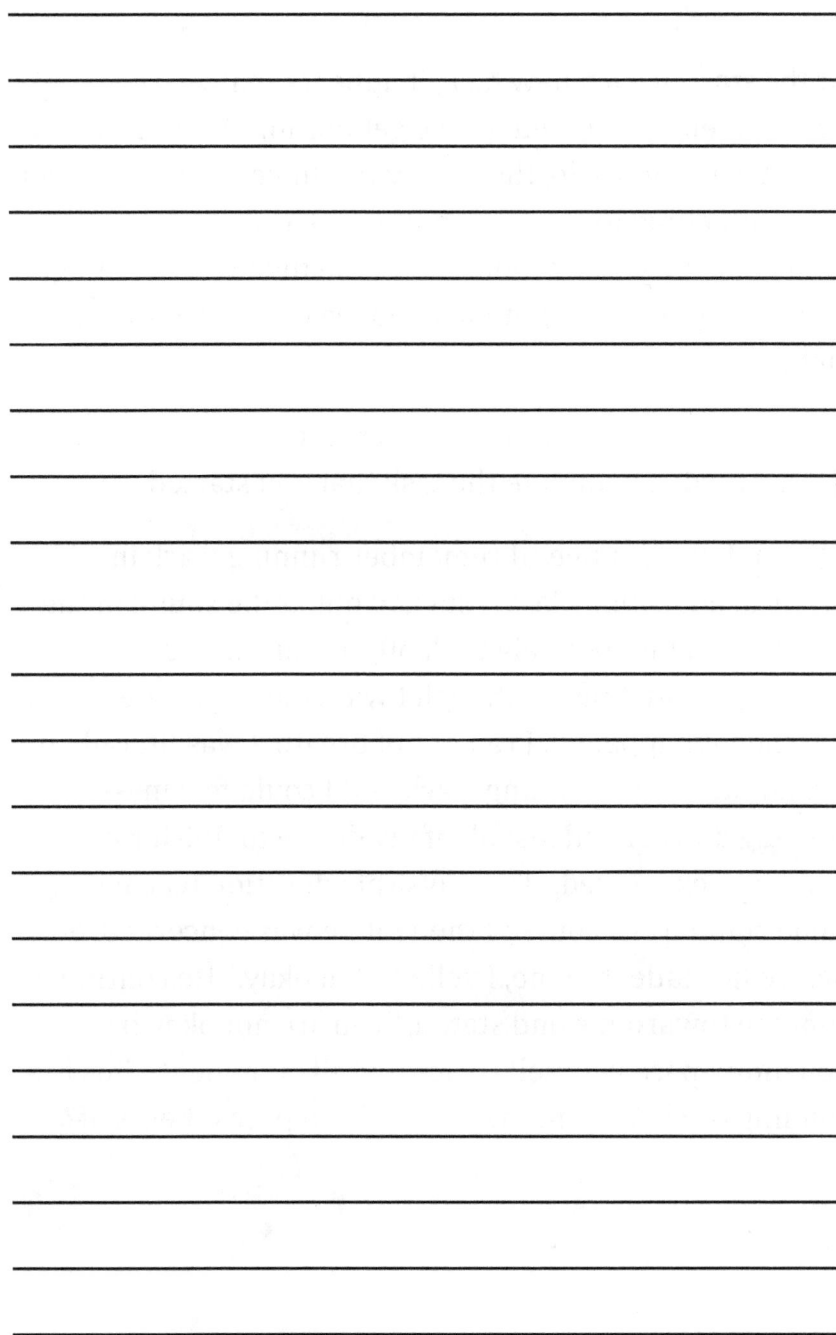

At the start of each new task, it appears that we are determined to complete it. We get our mind set on what it is that we want to do, then we work diligently for a certain amount of time to ensure that the task is done. This happens for a certain amount of time then we seem to get tired. After all, we are human and we do need a break, right?

In order to be unstoppable, you must be consistent and determined to complete the task that you started.

When I was younger, I remember running track in physical education class. I started out at the sound of the whistle and immediately took off, running as fast as I possibly could. I ran as though I was running for dear life. But then it happened. I ran out of breath. I was literally in the middle of the running track and I could feel myself slowing down. I had lost all of my desire to finish running and I was exhausted. The physical education teacher came running. Of course I thought he was concerned. So before he made it to me, I yelled, "I'm okay." He continued running toward me and stated, "You are not okay because you didn't pace yourself." Pace myself? I thought. This is a running track. Who in their right mind paces their self?

The coach told me to keep moving. He said even if I had to walk the rest of the way, I needed to continue along the running track. As I walked (and caught my breath), I saw everyone finishing. It was depressing and a little embarrassing. But I didn't give up. I finished.

Finishing what is started takes determination! We all have ideas, desires, and wants for our lives. But it means nothing if we don't take the time to see everything through to the end.

Determination

What task/idea are you determined to see through to the
end?

_____

_____

_____

_____

_____

_____

_____

_____

_____

_____

_____

_____

_____

_____

_____

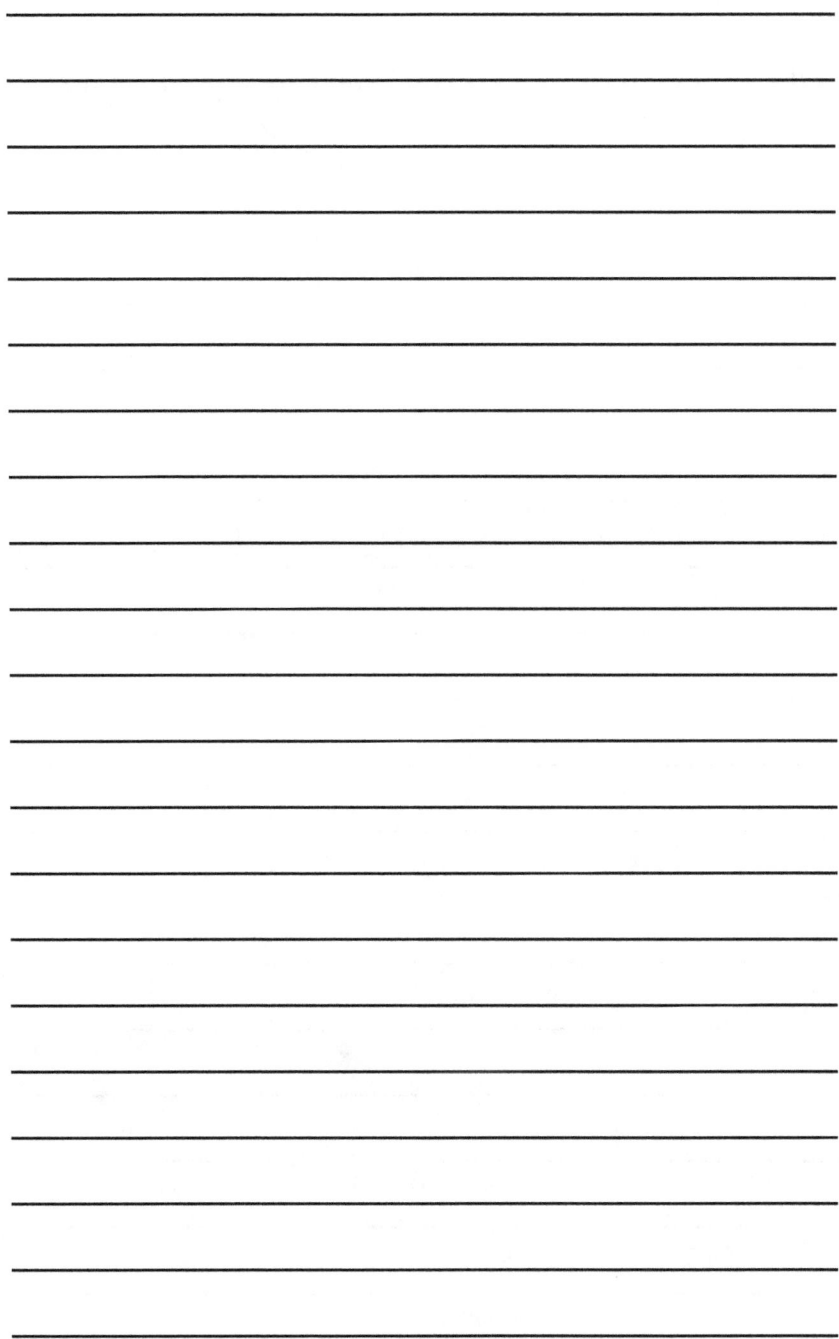

Will completion of your task help elevate you to the next level? If so, why or why not?

_____

_____

_____

_____

_____

_____

_____

_____

_____

_____

_____

_____

_____

_____

_____

_____

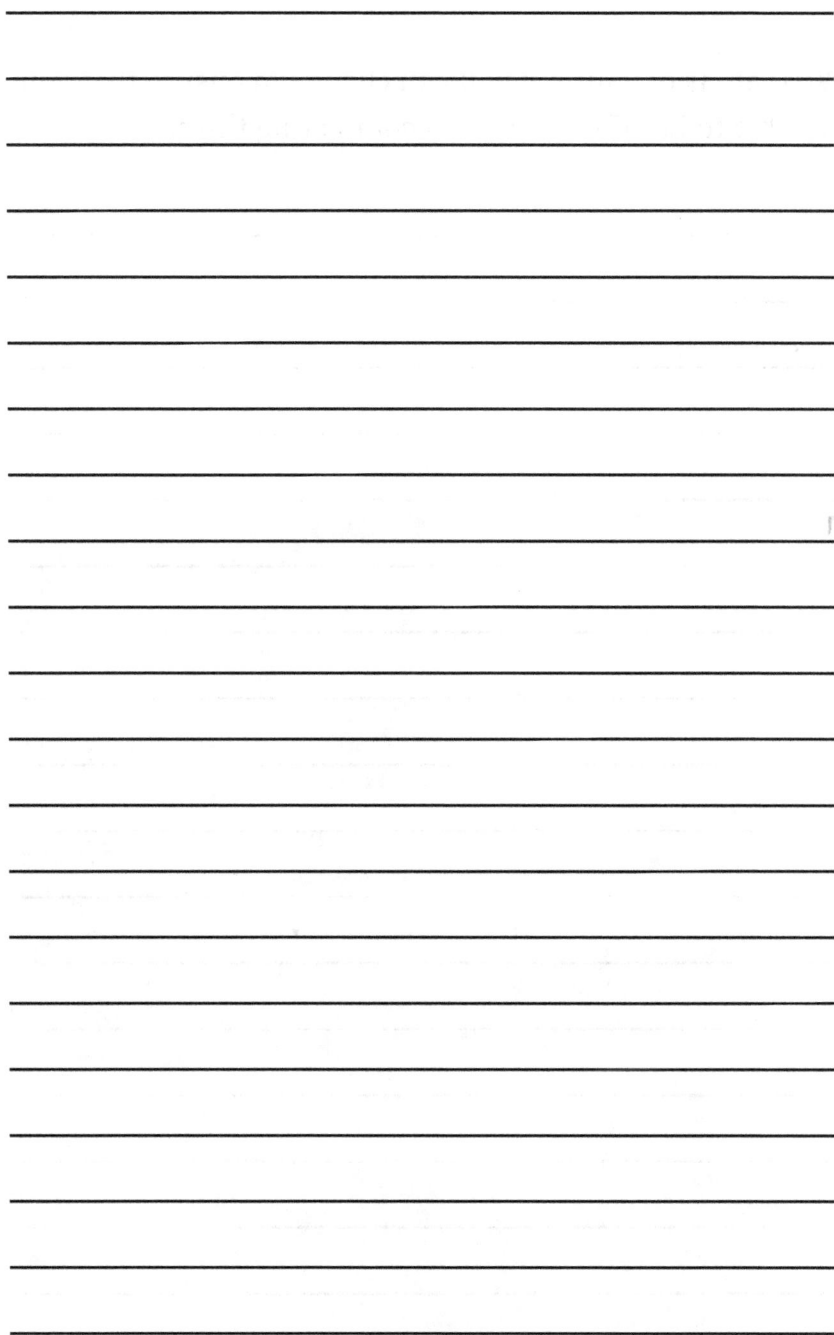

What areas of your life will you change to ensure that you are able to be consistent with completing this task?

_____

_____

_____

_____

_____

_____

_____

_____

_____

_____

_____

_____

_____

_____

_____

_____

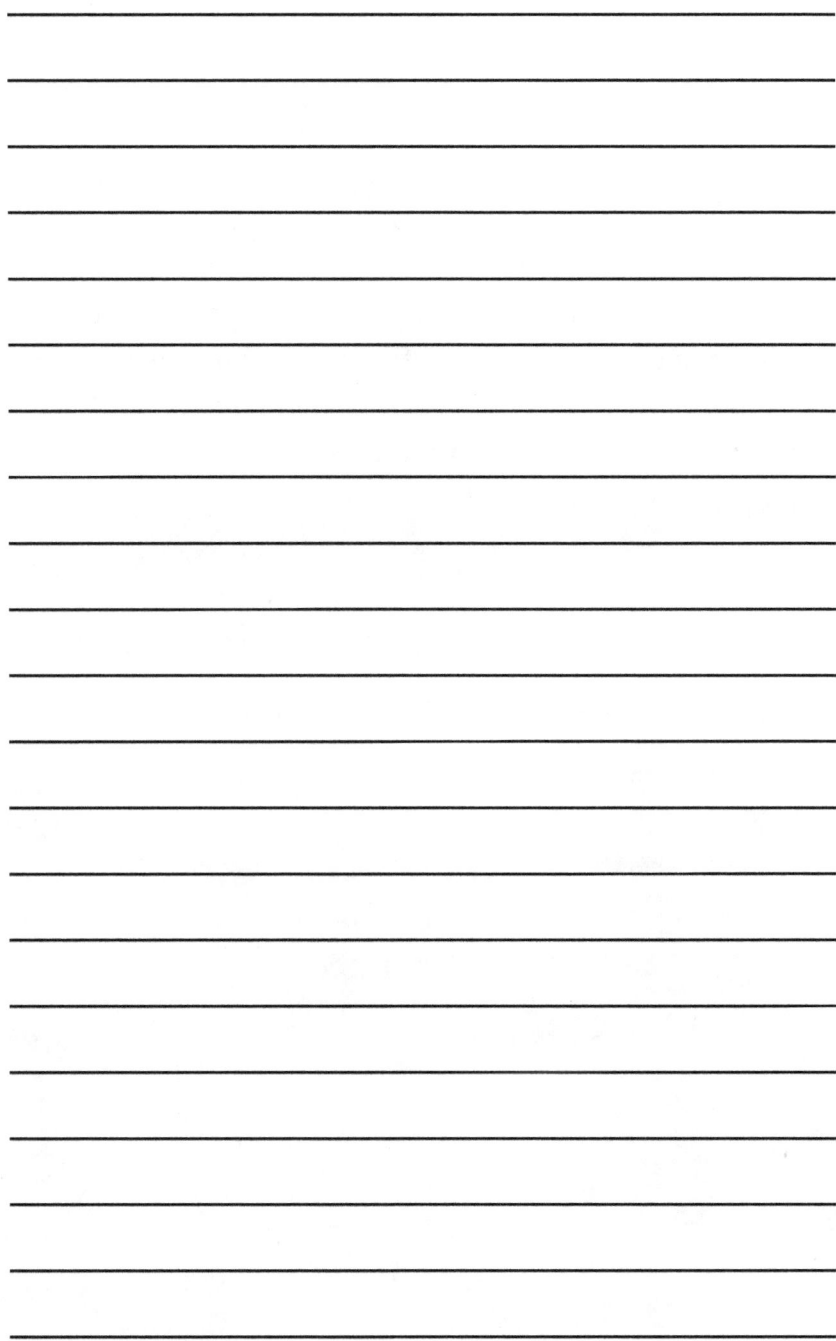

You have already completed the first few essential steps needed to succeed, stay focused and determined!

Determination is an essential element to your success. Nothing comes easy nor is anything that comes easy guaranteed to last. But if you are determined to continue working toward your dreams, they will turn into a reality right before your eyes.

Eliminating Self Desires

I have five hundred dollars in my handbag. I would love to drive to the shopping mall and purchase a new pair of designer shoes. I deserve to treat myself, right?

As much we all deserve to treat ourselves, when we have goals to reach, it is imperative that we are not spending all of our money and time on self-desires.

Unfortunately for me, I am an impulse buyer. I see something and before I can decide if I really need it, the items are already paid for, bagged, and waiting for me at the counter. It isn't until I arrive home and sit back and think about what I purchased, that I regret it. But by that time, I am too exhausted from shopping to go back to the store and return the items. In order to succeed we must be mindful of spending habits.

How much do you spend on handbags, designer shoes, and clothes each month?

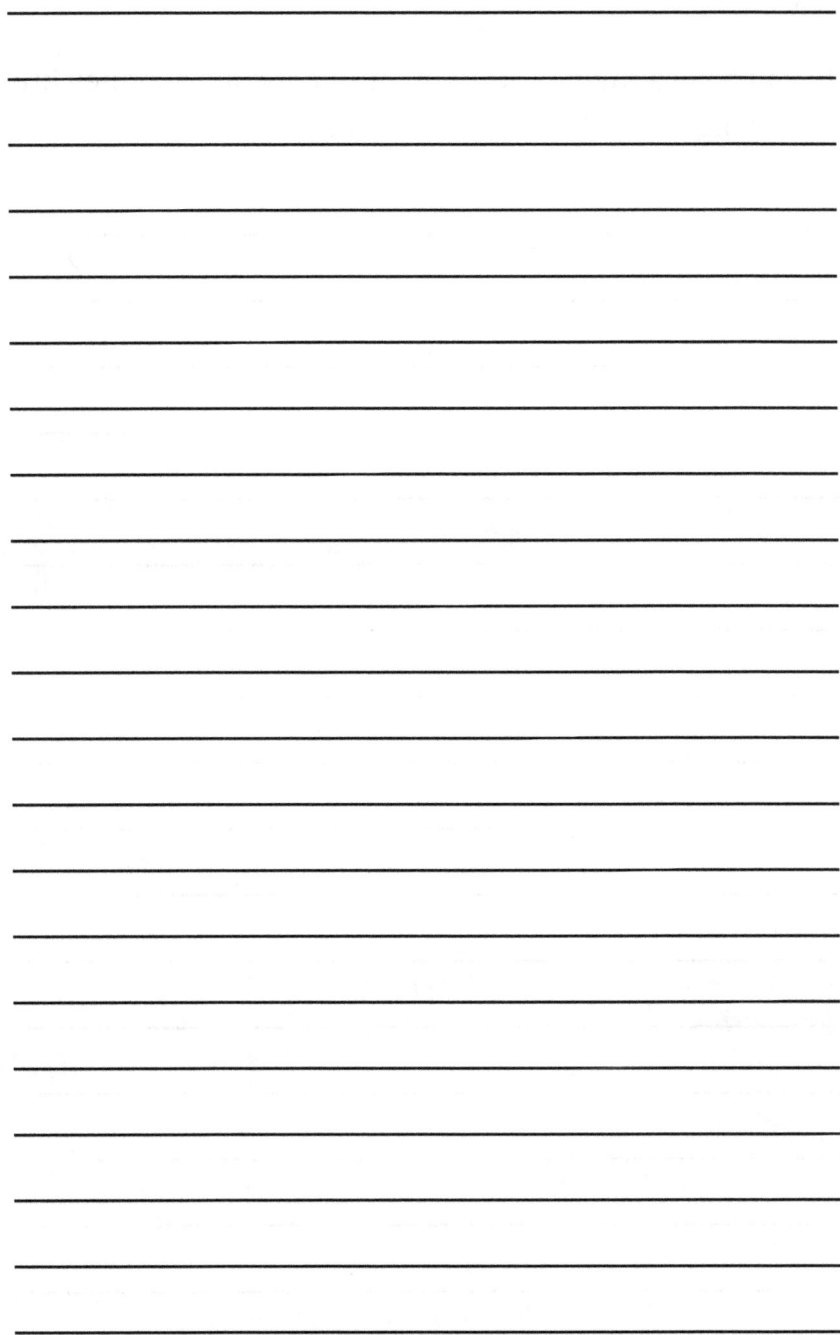

Do you have a savings account? If so how much money are you saving consistently each month?

_____

_____

_____

_____

_____

_____

_____

_____

_____

_____

_____

_____

_____

_____

_____

_____

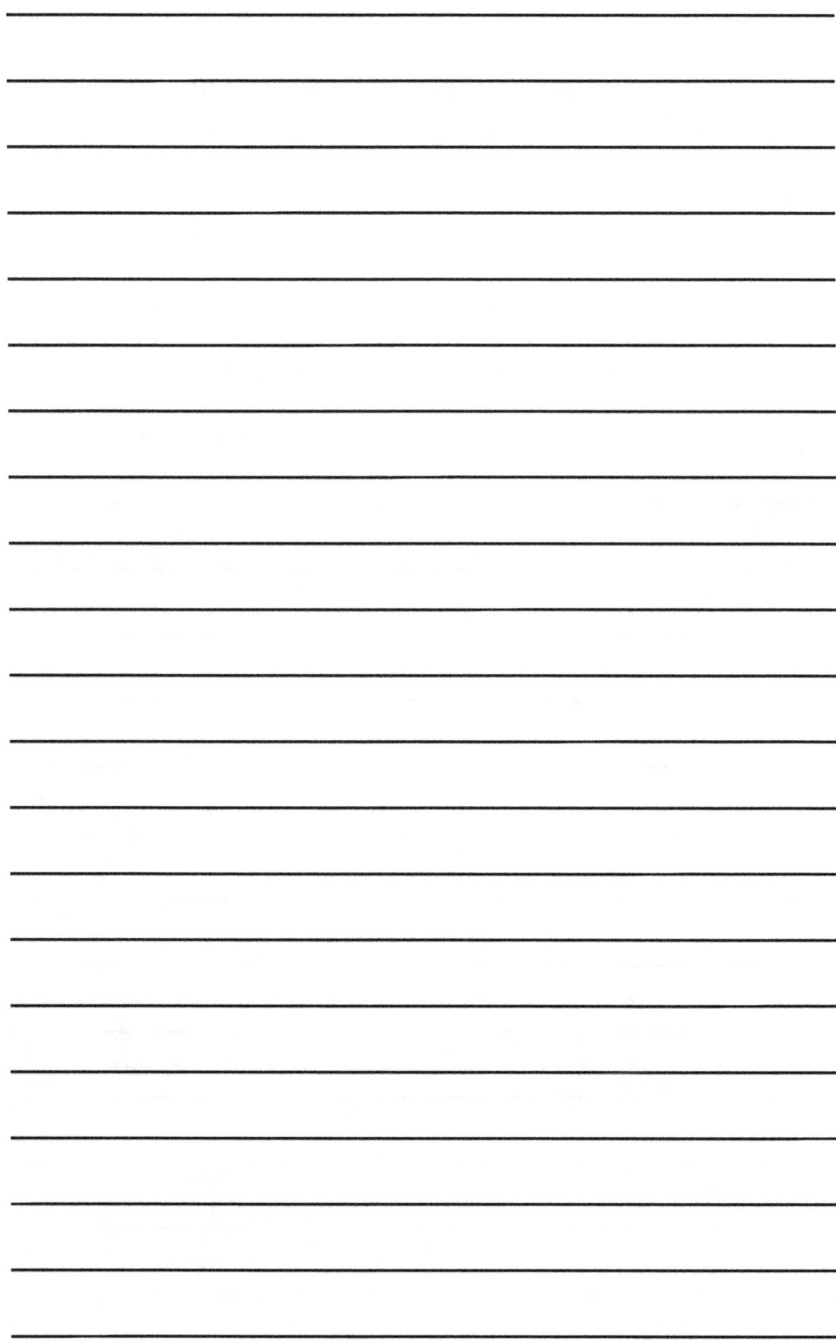

If your desire is to one day become an entrepreneur, how much are you investing toward your dream each month?

_____

_____

_____

_____

_____

_____

_____

_____

_____

_____

_____

_____

_____

_____

_____

Do you know that with a weekly savings of twenty dollars consistently for one year, you would have enough money saved to start a new business? Or, how about saving ten dollars each week for one year? With those funds, you would have enough money to buy an airplane ticket and travel to a new state for vacation.

We oftentimes limit ourselves in life. Not because we don't have the finances. But because we have wasted funds that were at our disposal. I literally ate out every day of the week for at least six months straight before I realized how much money I spent. It was $3,200.00 to be exact.

I could have paid a month's mortgage or tripled up on my car note and insurance, or even placed that money in my business account and invested in promotional items. But instead I used it to eat? Yes, we have to eat to survive but $3,200.00 worth of food in six months' time for one person? That is a bit extreme.

I started grocery shopping. I stopped eating out during the week. I learned to live on less and I am now thankful that I did. Not only do I have more 'coins' in the bank. But I am healthier and I have learned to implement self-control.

Self-control is needed when you are pressing towards being unstoppable. There will be times when you have to make decisions that may require you to change certain areas in your lifestyle in order to reach your goals.

Take time to reflect on your spending habits. Are your self-desires conflicting with you being unstoppable? Eliminate anything in your life that will cause you unhappiness in the future. You deserve to be unstoppable.

Embracing Rejection

If I had a nickel for every time I was rejected throughout my life, I would be sitting on a private island living the 'good life'.

Rejection can be defined as the dismissing or refusing of a proposal or idea. Though rejection may be painful, it is a necessary part of the growth process. Rejection can allow you to 'go harder' or simply throw in the towel and give up.

What rejections have you recently experienced?

_____

_____

_____

_____

_____

_____

_____

_____

_____

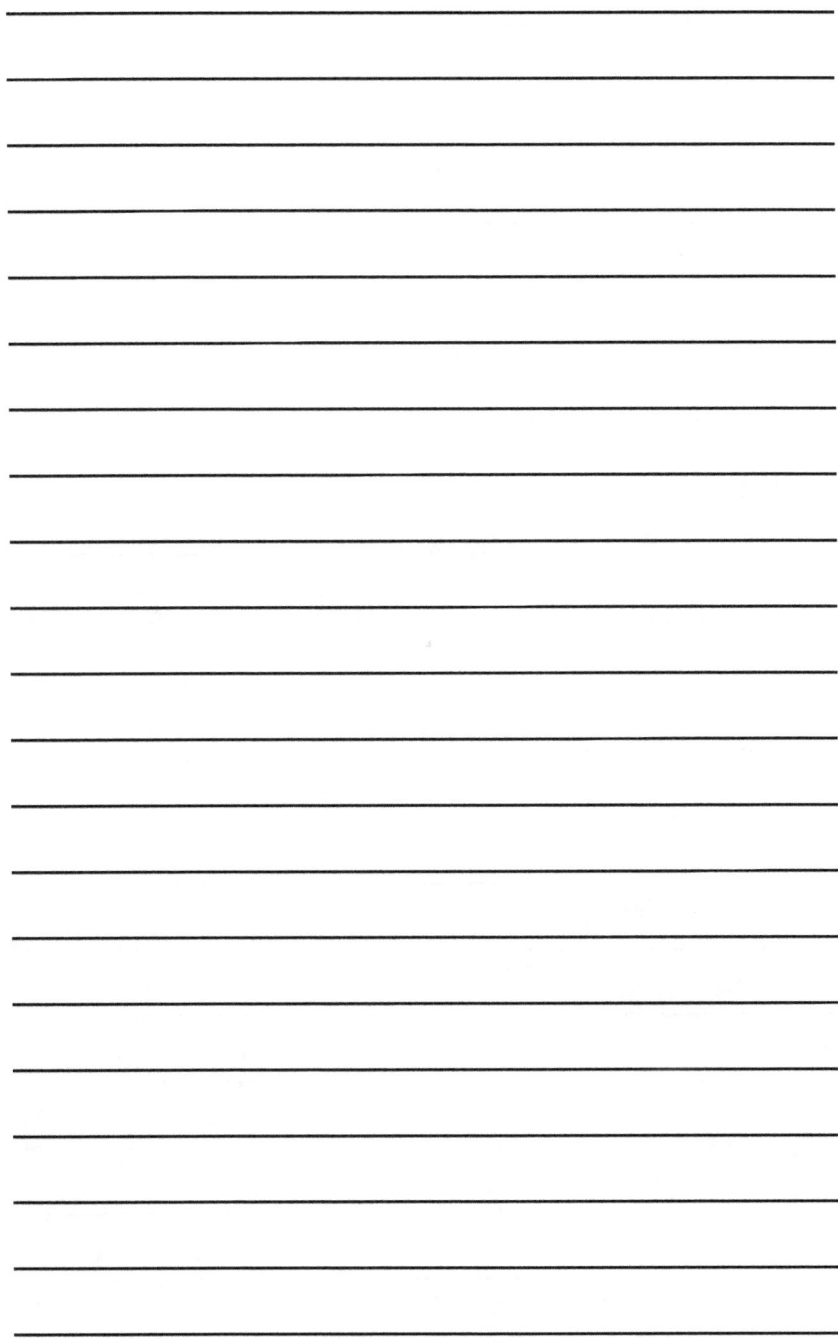

What is your initial reaction when faced with rejection?

_____

_____

_____

_____

_____

_____

_____

_____

_____

_____

_____

_____

_____

_____

_____

_____

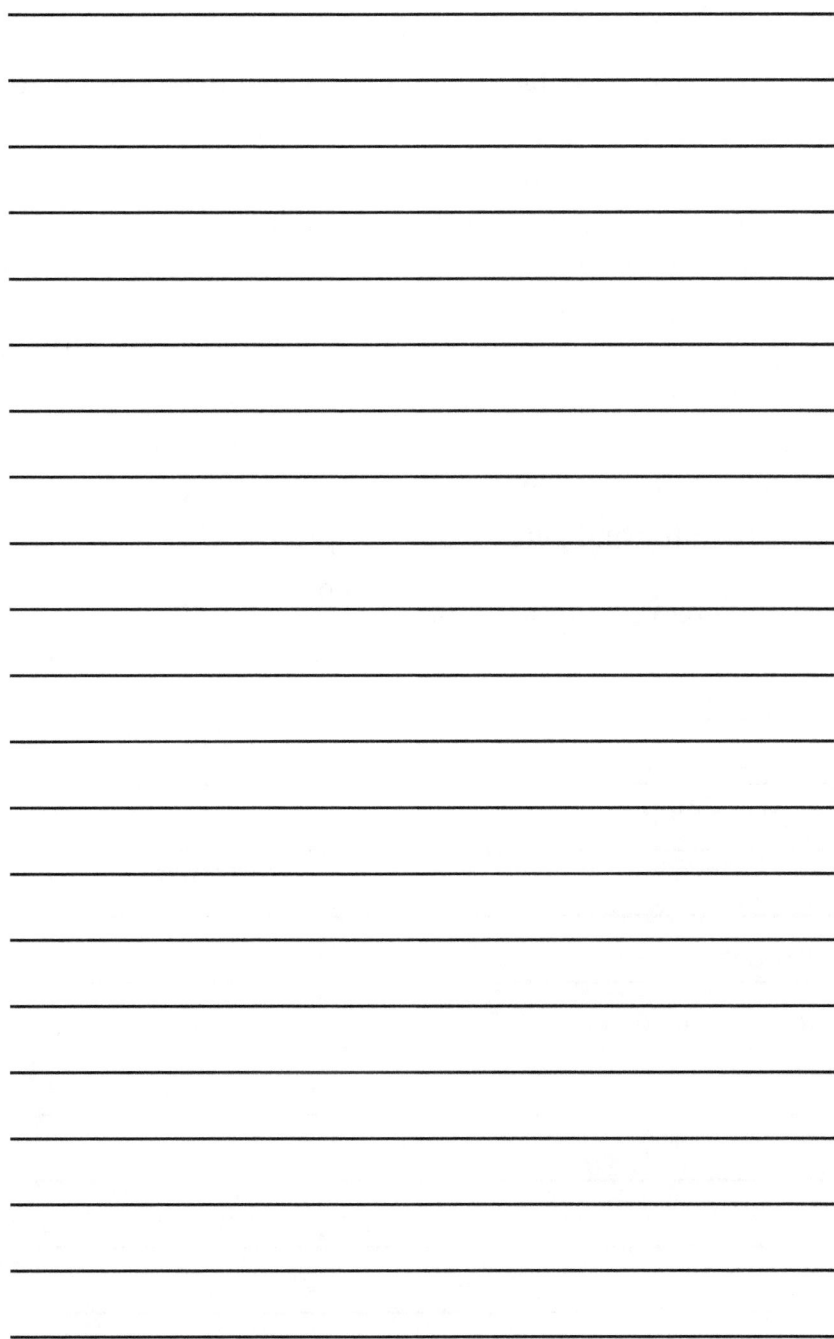

How we react to each situation speaks volumes about who we are as individuals. For instance, let's say you have been working on a project for the last three years. You finally pitch the idea of your project to a local investor. Less than five minutes into the pitch, the investor yells "NOT INTERESTED!"

You have a few options. You can choose to stand there with grace and dignity with the hope of finding a new investor. Or, you can storm out of the room crying, cursing and screaming and give up on your project.

Explain how you embrace rejections in your life.

_____

_____

_____

_____

_____

_____

_____

_____

_____

_____

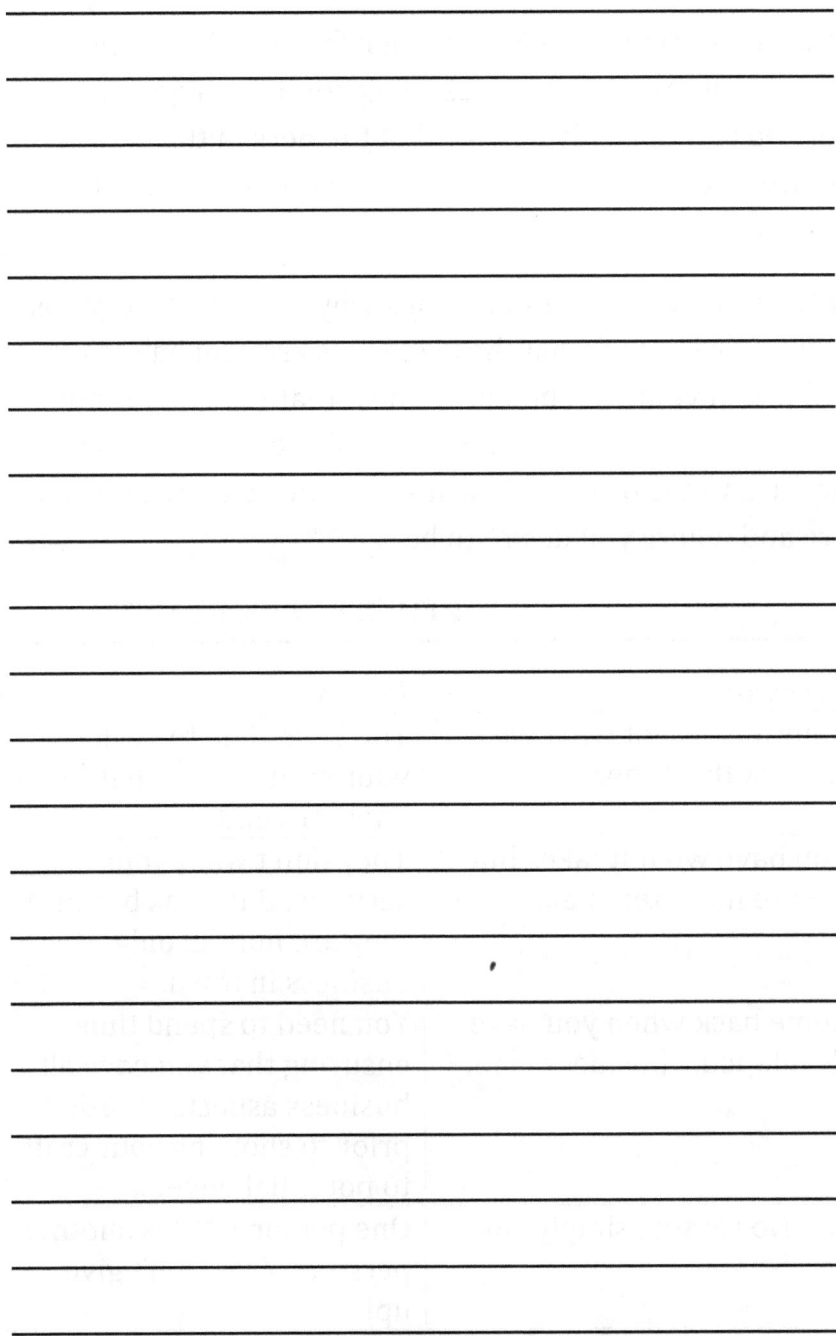

If your reaction is to give up when faced with rejection, you are not ready for success. Rejection is a huge part of life. Do you honestly believe that the person that you idolize the most in the world never had to withstand rejection?

There are a number of reasons why you may be rejected. But regardless of what those reasons are, you have to believe in yourself enough to know that rejection is not the end. In fact, it is the beginning. You have more time to go back to the drawing board and re-evaluate where you are and where you desire to be.

REJECTION VS. REALITY

Rejection	Reality
Your idea is not what we want at this time.	You have time to perfect your craft and pitch it to another vendor.
You have what it takes but we are not interested.	They don't want your services. But relax because they are not the only business in town.
Come back when you have developed a business plan.	You need to spend time ensuring that you have all business aspects in order prior to showing your craft to potential buyers.
No- No reason, simply No.	One person's NO is another person's YES- Don't give up!

Rejection today can turn into a yes tomorrow. Don't ever give up simply because someone rejects you. Not everyone can see the vision that was given to you. You have to give birth to your ideas, desires, hopes, and dreams and turn them into reality.

The vision doesn't die unless you allow it to. No one and nothing can stop you once you make the conscious decision to be unstoppable.

Self-Investment

How have you invested in yourself?

_____

_____

_____

_____

_____

_____

_____

_____

_____

_____

_____

_____

_____

_____

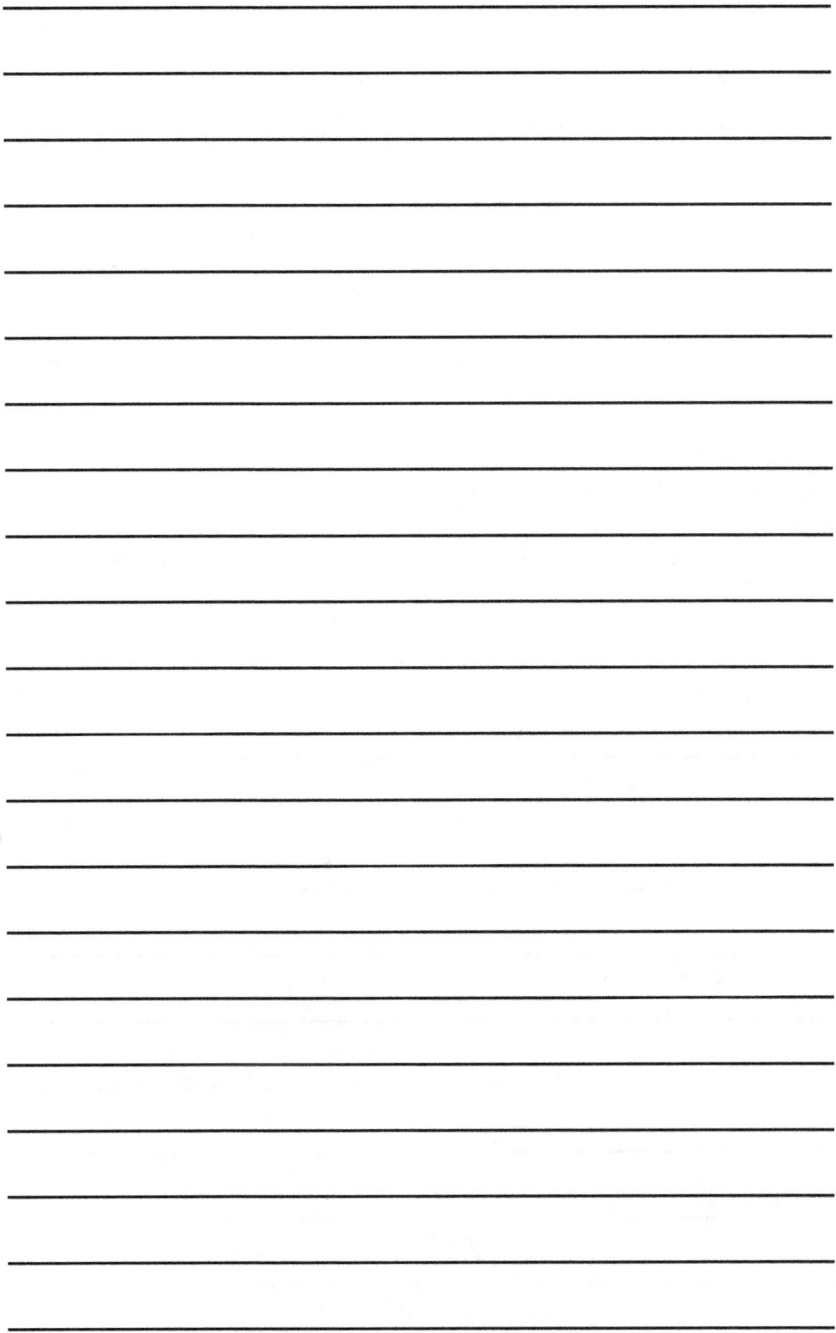

What resources do you have at your disposal that you can utilize to aid you towards investing in yourself?

_____

_____

_____

_____

_____

_____

_____

_____

_____

_____

_____

_____

_____

_____

_____

_____

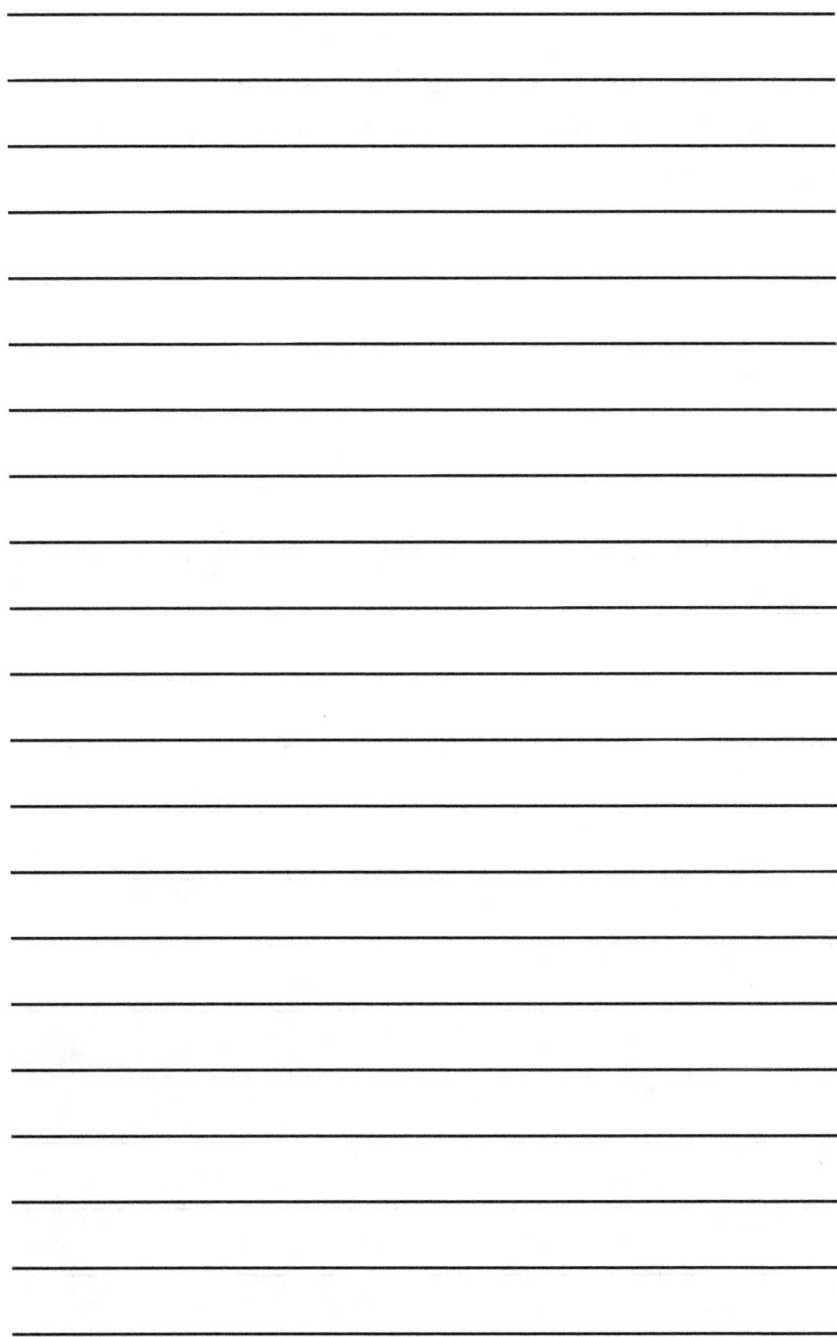

What hinders you from being able to self-invest? What changes are you willing to make at this very moment to begin investing in yourself?

_____

_____

_____

_____

_____

_____

_____

_____

_____

_____

_____

_____

_____

_____

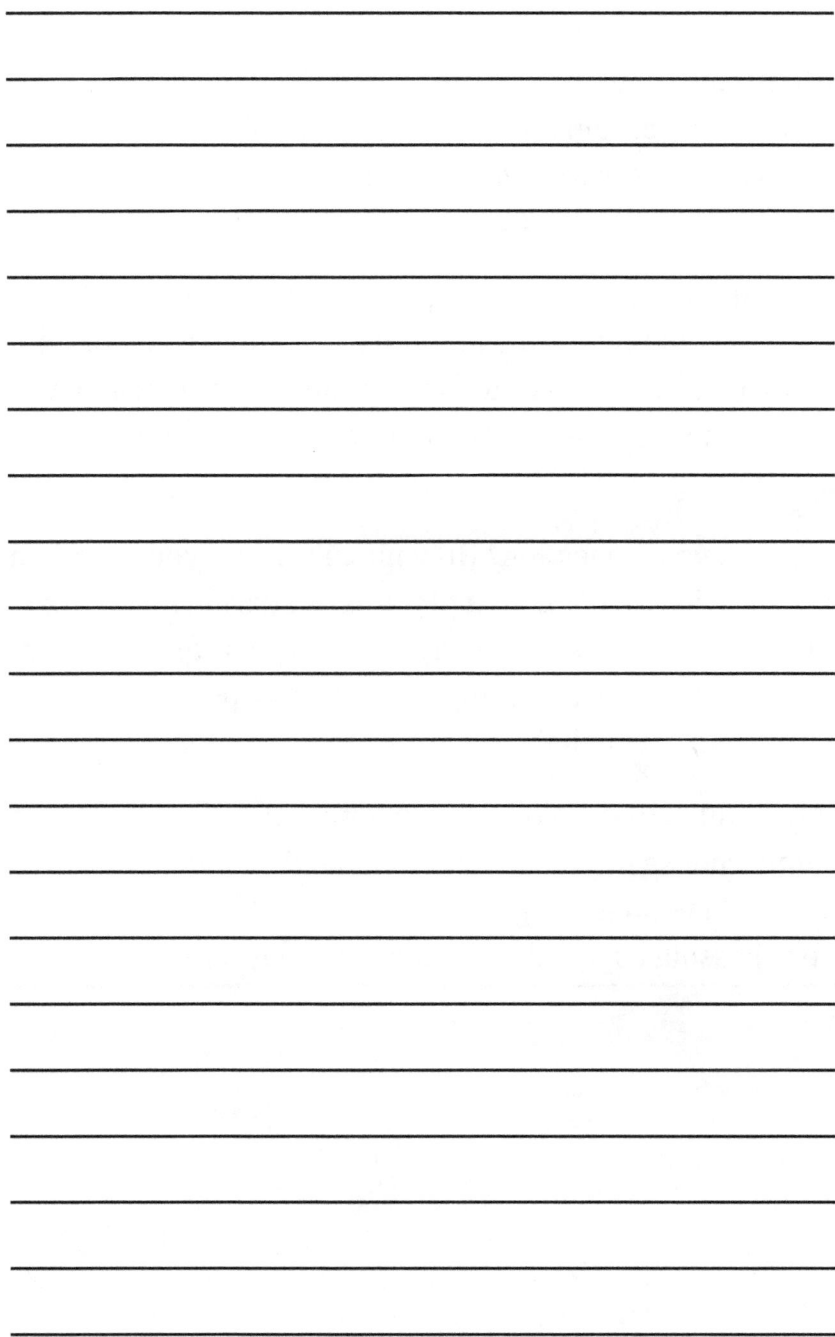

Oftentimes, when we hear the words 'self- invest,' we immediately assume that money is involved. However, that is not necessarily the case. Investing in yourself goes beyond financial means.

One of the greatest investments that you can make for yourself is to invest time for yourself. I know you work 40 hours a week. You have to pick up the children from day care, prepare dinner, and complete chores all while maintaining your sanity.

Can I ask you a question? How much time do you spend on social media. . .from Liking pictures to sharing links? That is time spent that is not in any way, shape or form helping you (unless you are running a business or promoting through social media).

My point is that we do have time to self-invest. We simply choose not to. Instead we spend countless hours on social media lurking at what the world is doing while life is passing us by. . .hour after hour; day after day.

In order to be unstoppable, you have to refrain from watching life pass you by and start investing in yourself. Schedule a certain time every day (set an alarm if needed) for a designated timeframe to invest in you. What do you like to do? Where do you see yourself in the next five years? Do you want to one day be a CEO of your own company? It is time to allow your desires to manifest....

Take a few moments to decide what you want the rest of your life to consist of; include every aspect of your life. Write down specific details of your future desires.

_____

_____

_____

_____

_____

_____

_____

_____

_____

_____

_____

_____

_____

_____

_____

Now that you have written down your 'future' life on paper, go out and make your desire a reality. No one knows what tomorrow will bring. But you do have the ability to choose to be unstoppable.

_____

_____

_____

_____

_____

_____

_____

_____

_____

_____

_____

_____

_____

_____

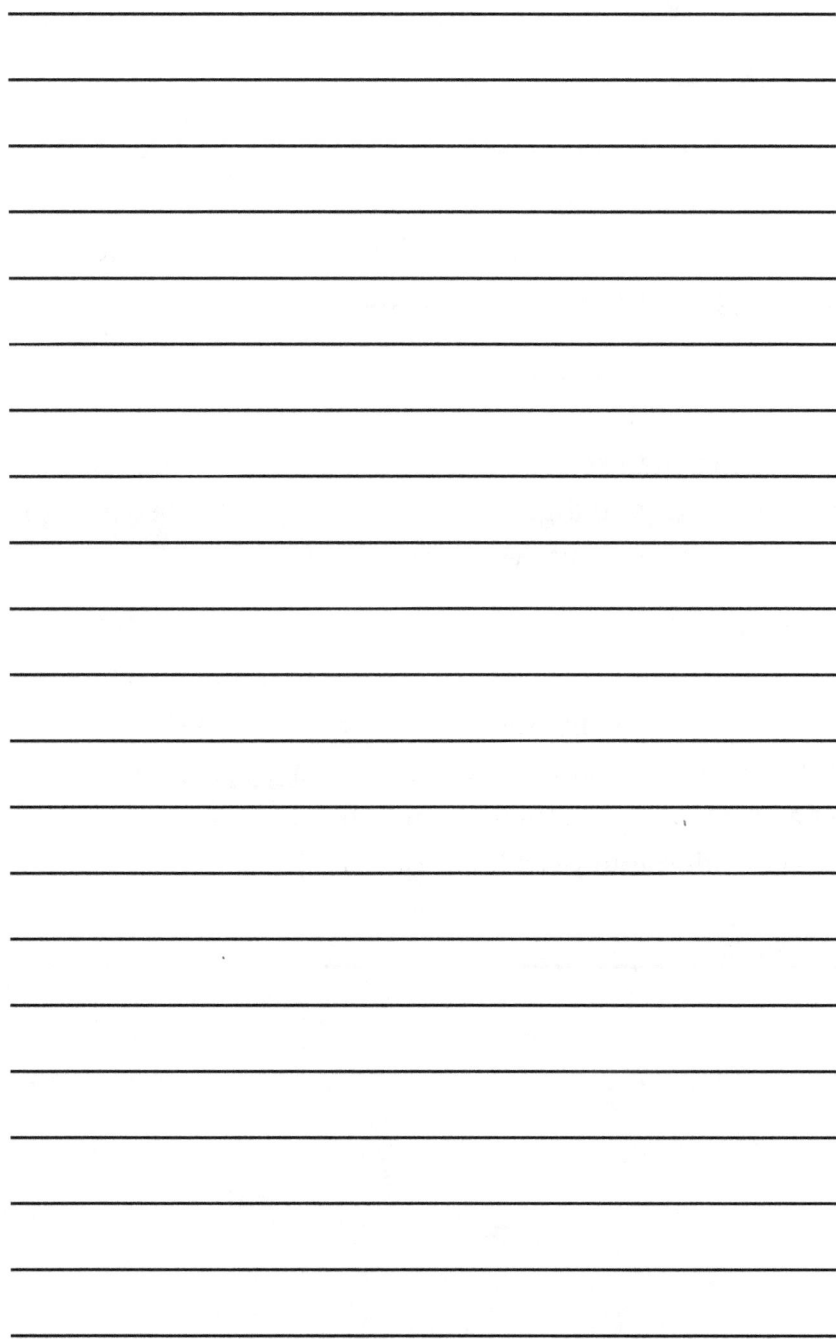

Goal-Getter

It is no secret that men refer to women who are only after money as 'gold diggers'. This phrase has been around for years. In fact, it is so common that people have identified specific groups of women as such.

These women 'supposedly' want money and aren't ashamed of it. They make that fact known when they approach a man so that there is no confusion along the way. If these 'gold diggers' can be straight forward and go after what they want, what's stopping you?

Instead of being a 'gold digger,' I am challenging you to become a 'Goal-Getter'! A goal-getter is someone who is so invested in achieving their goals that they are straight forward, to the point, and even a bit pushy. They know what they want and they are not afraid to go after it! Do you consider yourself a 'Goal-Getter'?

What have you done within the past 24 hours that would give you the privilege of calling yourself a Goal-Getter?

_____

_____

_____

_____

_____

_____

_____

_____

_____

_____

_____

_____

_____

_____

_____

Goal-Getters are always hustling. They know what they want and they don't stop until they get it. Is it easy being a Goal-Getter? No, of course not. If it was, then everyone would become one. The reality is that it takes hard work and self-discipline in order to stay on track and reach every goal that you have established for yourself.

Goal-Getters must face adversity. But they know that the only thing that matters is reaching the goal that they originally set. Regardless of how long it takes and what mountains that have to be climbed, they can't stop until the goal is reached.

Do you have what it takes to be a goal-getter?

_____

_____

_____

_____

_____

_____

_____

_____

_____

_____

_____

_____

_____

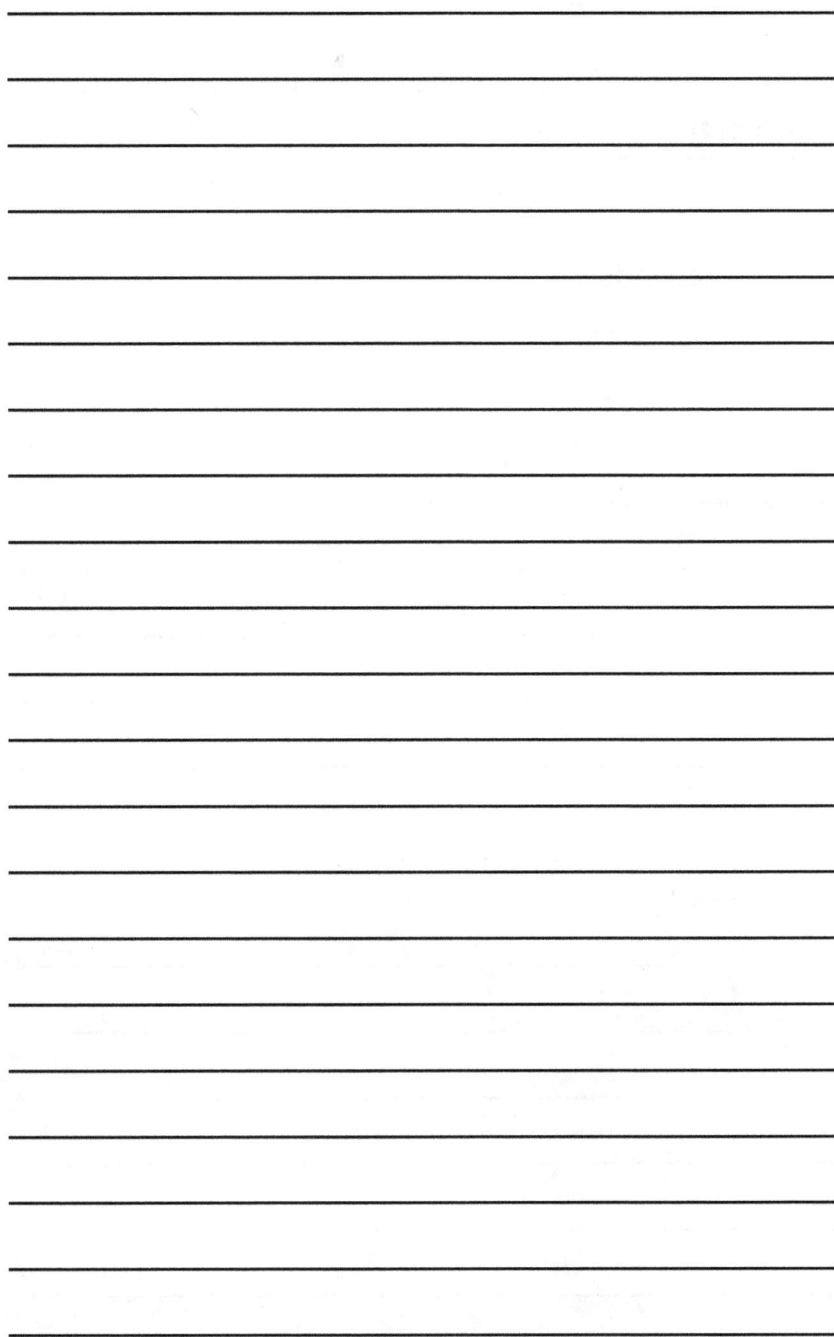

There are essential qualities instilled in Goal-Getters. Which of the qualities listed below do you possess?

1. Resourceful
2. Independent
3. Open-minded
4. Confident
5. Persistent

_____

_____

_____

_____

_____

_____

_____

_____

_____

_____

_____

_____

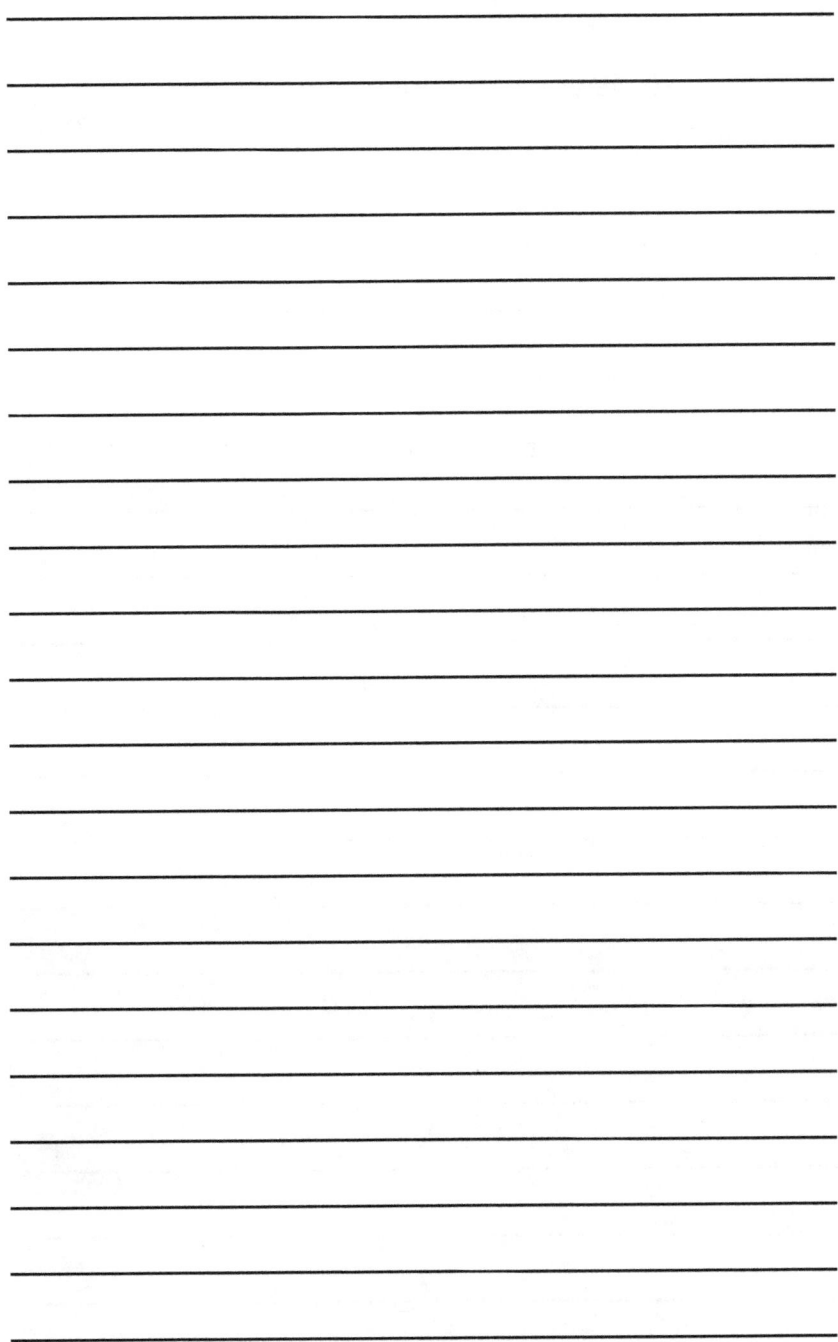

List action steps you can take to become a
Goal-Getter.

_____

_____

_____

_____

_____

_____

_____

_____

_____

_____

_____

_____

_____

_____

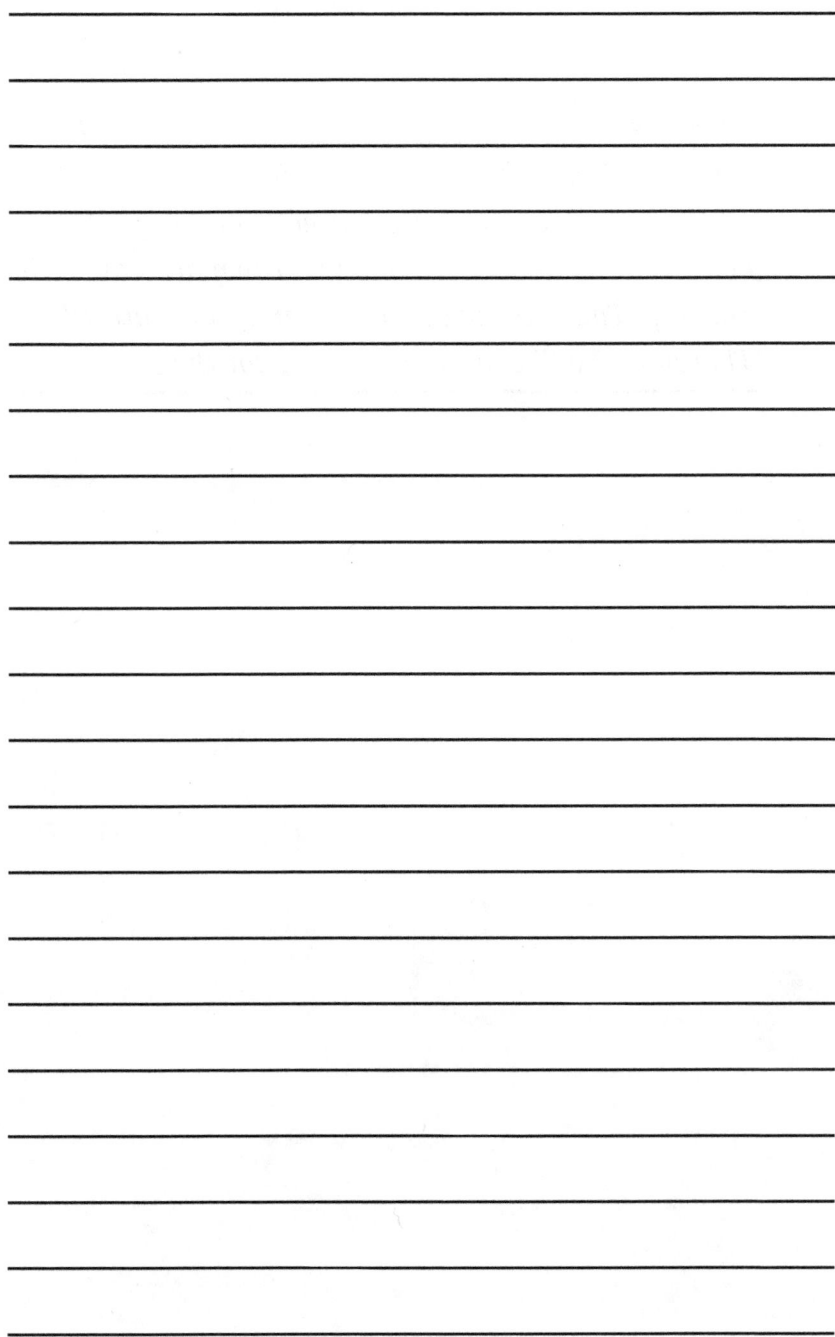

My name is _____ *and I can proudly say that I am a Goal-Getter. I laugh at adversity and look rejection directly in the eye. I know that no matter what gets thrown my way, I will not stop. That's because what I can do is limitless! Therefore, I will continue reaching for the sky!*

Motivation

What motivates you to get out of bed each morning?

_____

_____

_____

_____

_____

_____

_____

_____

_____

_____

_____

_____

_____

_____

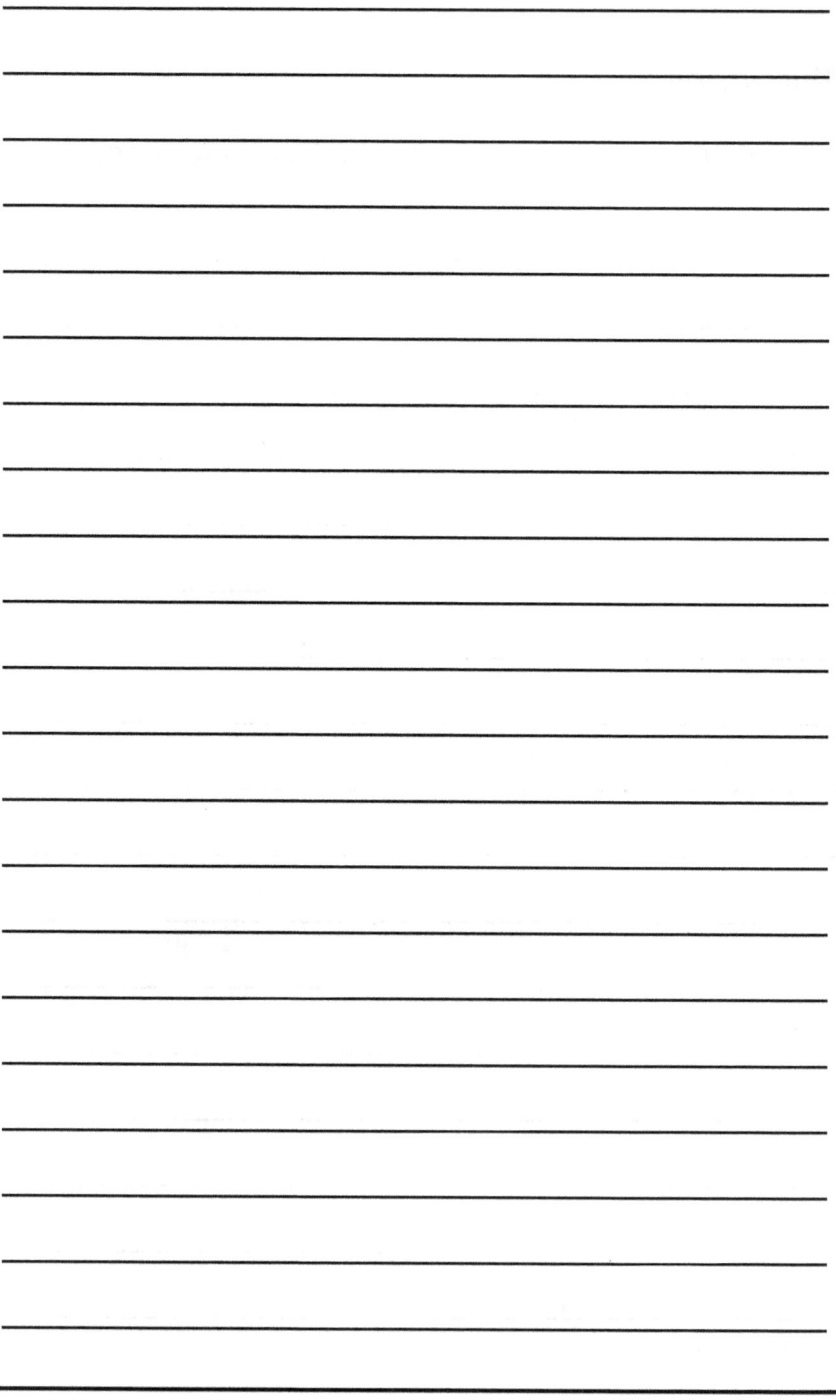

Allow what motivates you to become your muse. Regardless of who or what it is, allow what motivates you to inspire you through your journey. During those days of disappointment, use your muse to empower you to continue pushing forward to becoming unstoppable.

If your muse is a child, find a photo of them doing something silly. Attach it to a place that you always look so that you can be reminded that there are things more important than whatever disappointment you faced that day.

If your muse is an actor/actress, tear out a description of work that they have completed so that you can see that giving up is not an option. If they can do great works, so can you.

_____

_____

_____

_____

_____

_____

_____

_____

_____

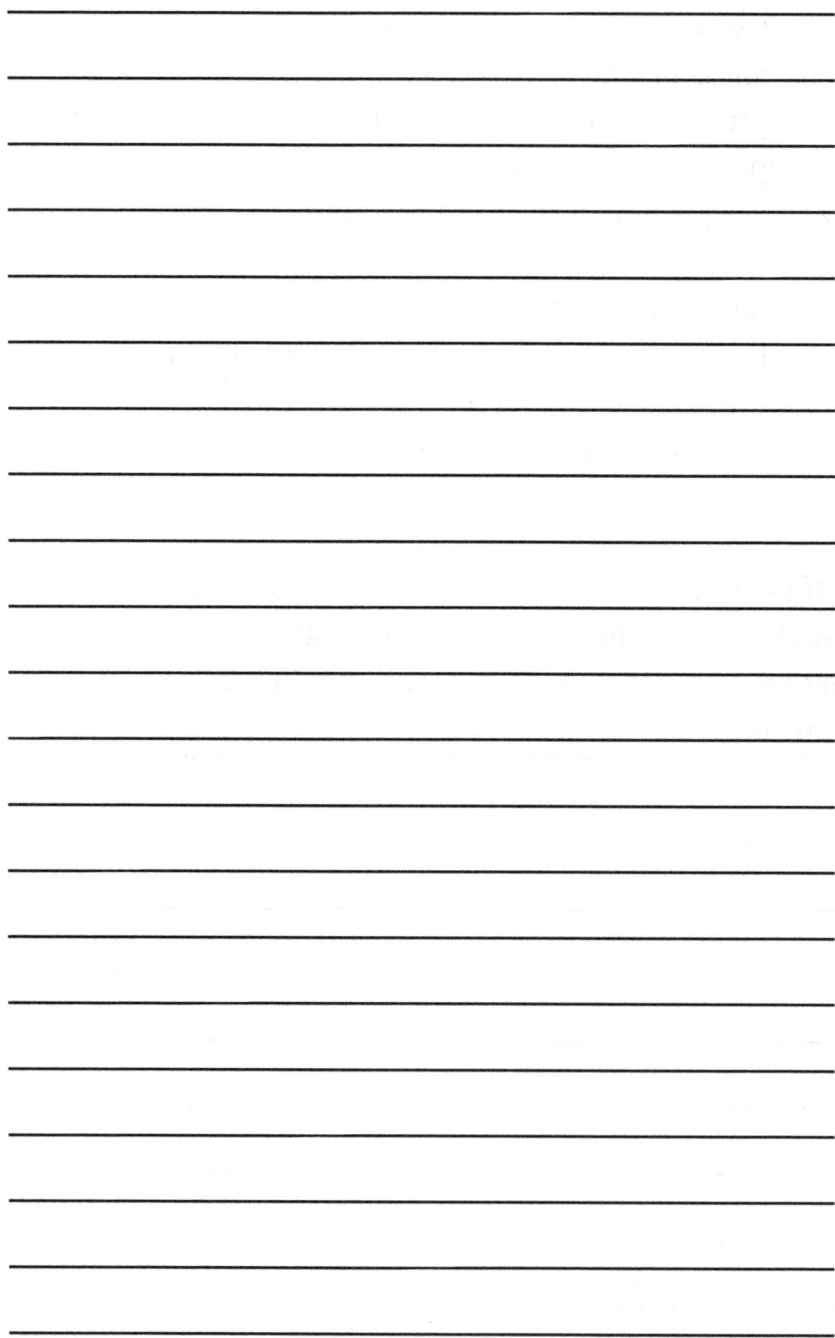

Motivational Tips

1. Spend time learning new things.
2. Write down ideas throughout the day that are positive.
3. Start a motivation bucket.
4. Set aside time each day to reflect.
5. Find support from like-minded people.

_____

_____

_____

_____

_____

_____

_____

_____

_____

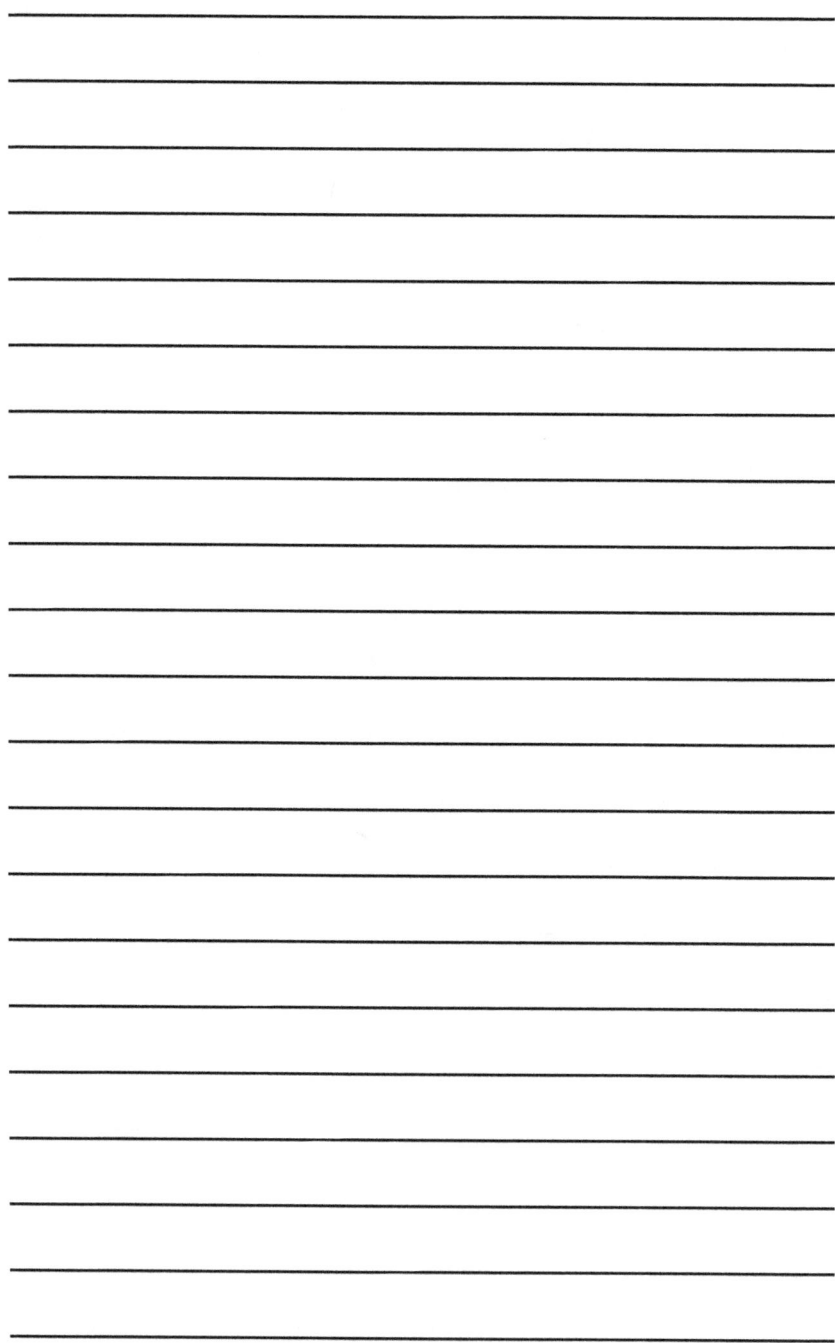

Motivational Muse

1. Children/Spouse
2. Artifacts
3. Famous Person
4. Literature
5. Departed Loved Ones

Daily Reflection

Sometimes, we are so caught up in what we want to achieve that we forget to take the time to reflect on what we have already accomplished. I know you have goals to reach. But in the midst of everything, you need to understand that what you have already accomplished should be acknowledged.

During the process of becoming unstoppable, you will have days where you may want to give up and just call it quits. During those days, it is important that you have a written journal of everything that you have already accomplished. Whether your accomplishment is winning an award or simply being the shoulder that someone needed. It should be documented.

Take a few moments to consider all that you have done thus far.
Let's learn to celebrate ourselves and acknowledge what we do on a daily basis.

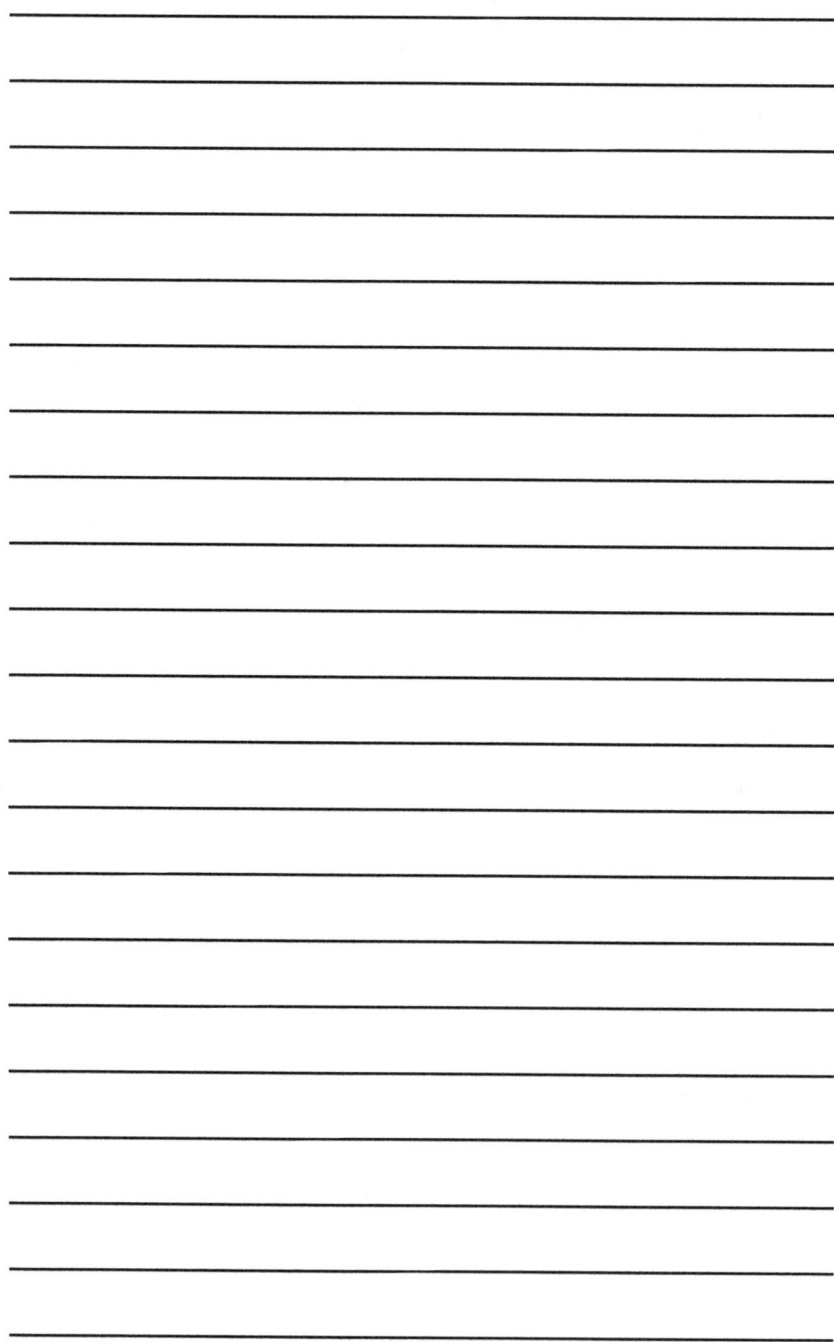

Take the time to reflect and journal where you are in your
life.

_____

_____

_____

_____

_____

_____

_____

_____

_____

_____

_____

_____

_____

_____

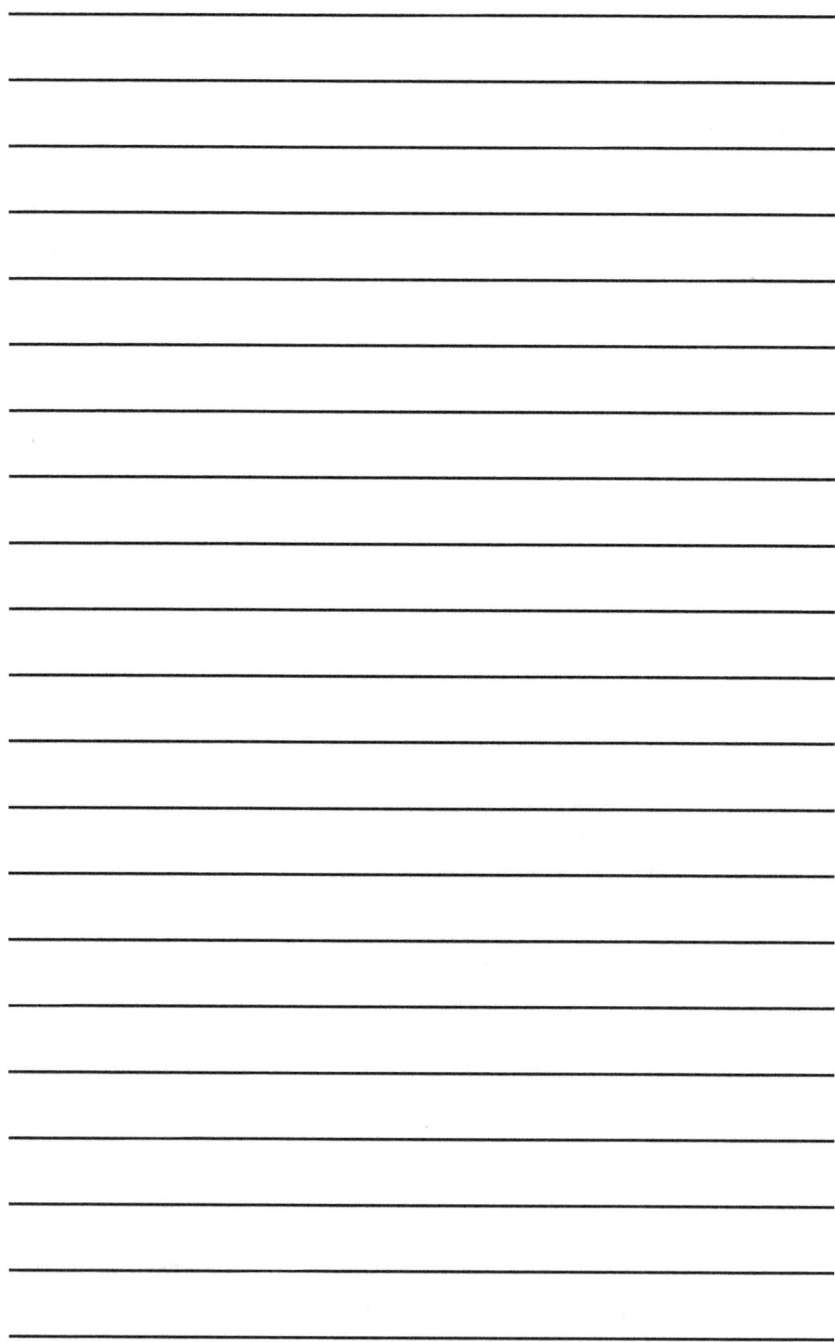

Based on what you previously wrote, what are the key words that stand out?

_____

_____

_____

_____

_____

_____

_____

_____

_____

_____

_____

_____

_____

_____

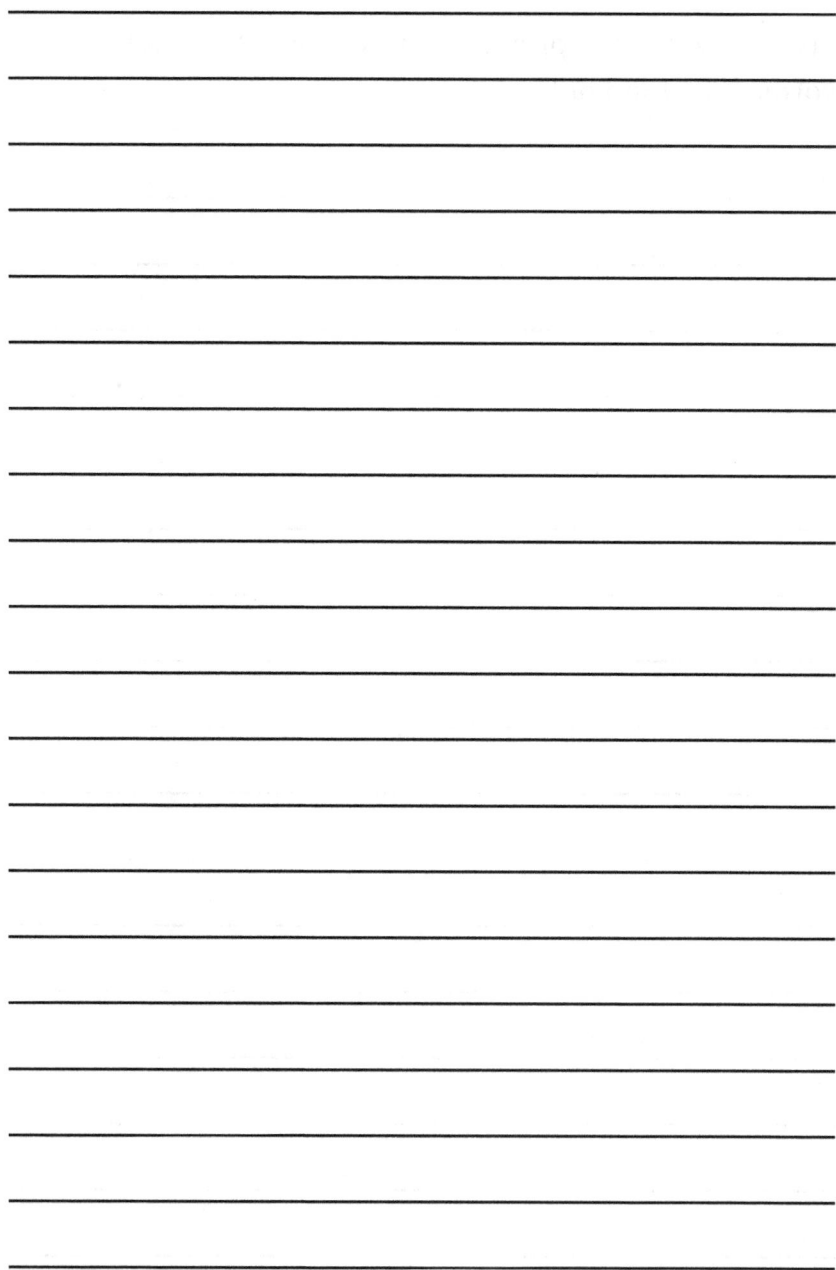

The words that stand out most should be used as your road map to guide you to the next level of your life. Look at the words below, circle the words that STAND out.

New House   Family

Business Venture

Free Time   Vacation

Financial Freedom

Why did the words circled stand out?

Use the key words from what stood out from your reflection along with the circled words and create ways to allow the words to become part of your reality. Reflect on the key words regularly and soon you will be unstoppable.

_____

_____

_____

_____

_____

_____

_____

_____

_____

_____

_____

_____

_____

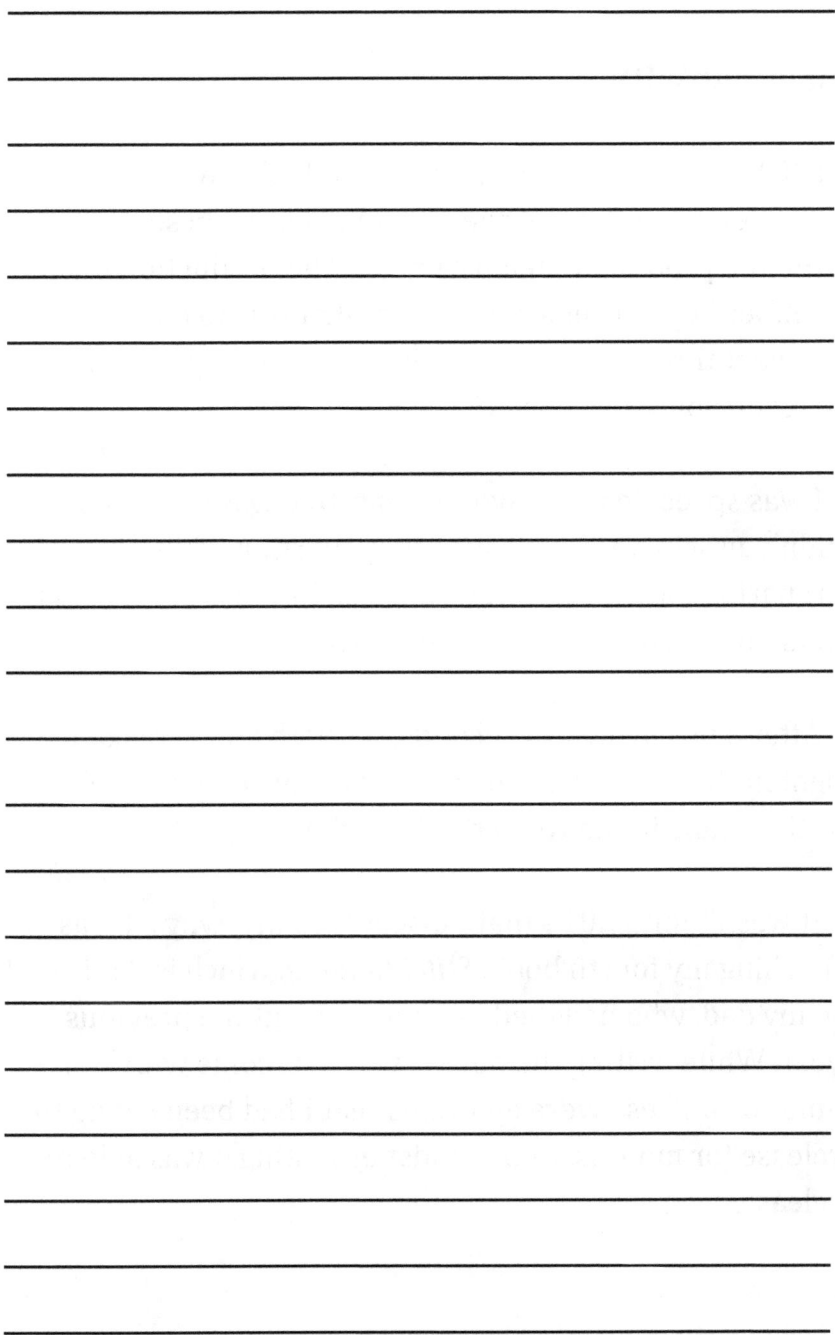

Find your WHY

In 2012, I was sitting in an interview lobby, waiting to be interviewed to discuss one of my books, when someone from the production team came in. The production team member began preparing me for what was to come. Once we went through formalities, he asked me a question. 'Why do you write books?'

I was speechless for two reasons. One was because I didn't anticipate being asked that question while preparing for the interview and also because at that very moment, I had no idea how to answer.

After a few awkward seconds, we both laughed just to lighten the mood. Then he walked away and I was left sitting alone in the room thinking about my 'why'.

It wasn't until 2014 that I discovered my 'why'. I was finishing my fourth book, *Still Standing*, which is dedicated to my dad, who had died in a car accident the previous year. While writing the book, I was overcome with emotions. These were emotions that I had been trying to release for months. In the midst of writing, I was able to release.

I felt as though I was free. It was at that moment I realized 'why' I write. I write because writing gives me a sense of freedom. It is therapeutic and allows me to be free with no limitations or boundaries. I write because not only does it benefit me. But I know that there are others who are hurting and seek inspiration through written words. Two years later I finally found my 'why'.

Have you discovered your 'Why'?

_____

_____

_____

_____

_____

_____

_____

_____

_____

_____

_____

_____

_____

_____

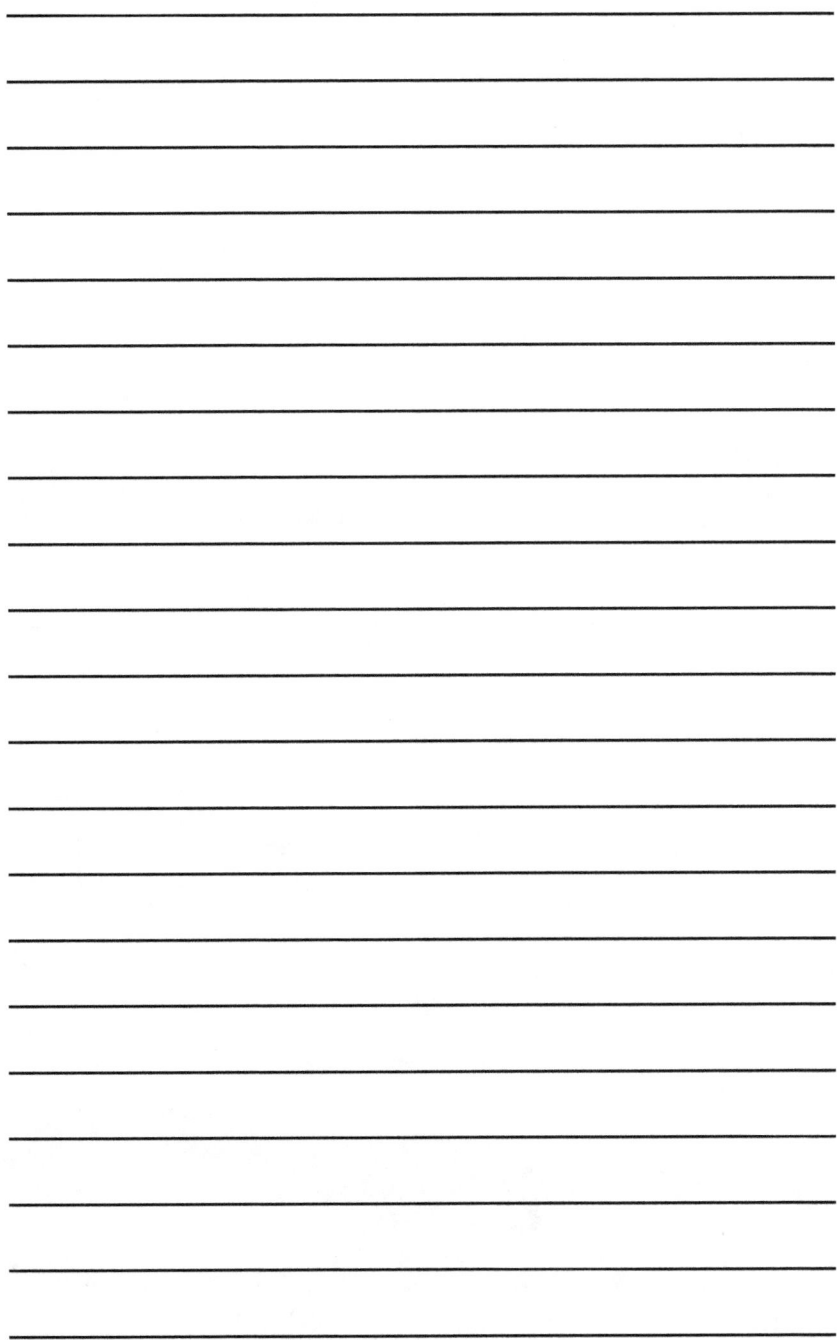

What word below describes how you feel at this very moment?

Emotional
Happy
Doubtful
Excited
Scared
Hopeful

Take a moment and think about what you are passionate about then write it down. I am passionate about....

_____

_____

_____

_____

_____

_____

_____

_____

_____

_____

_____

_____

_____

_____

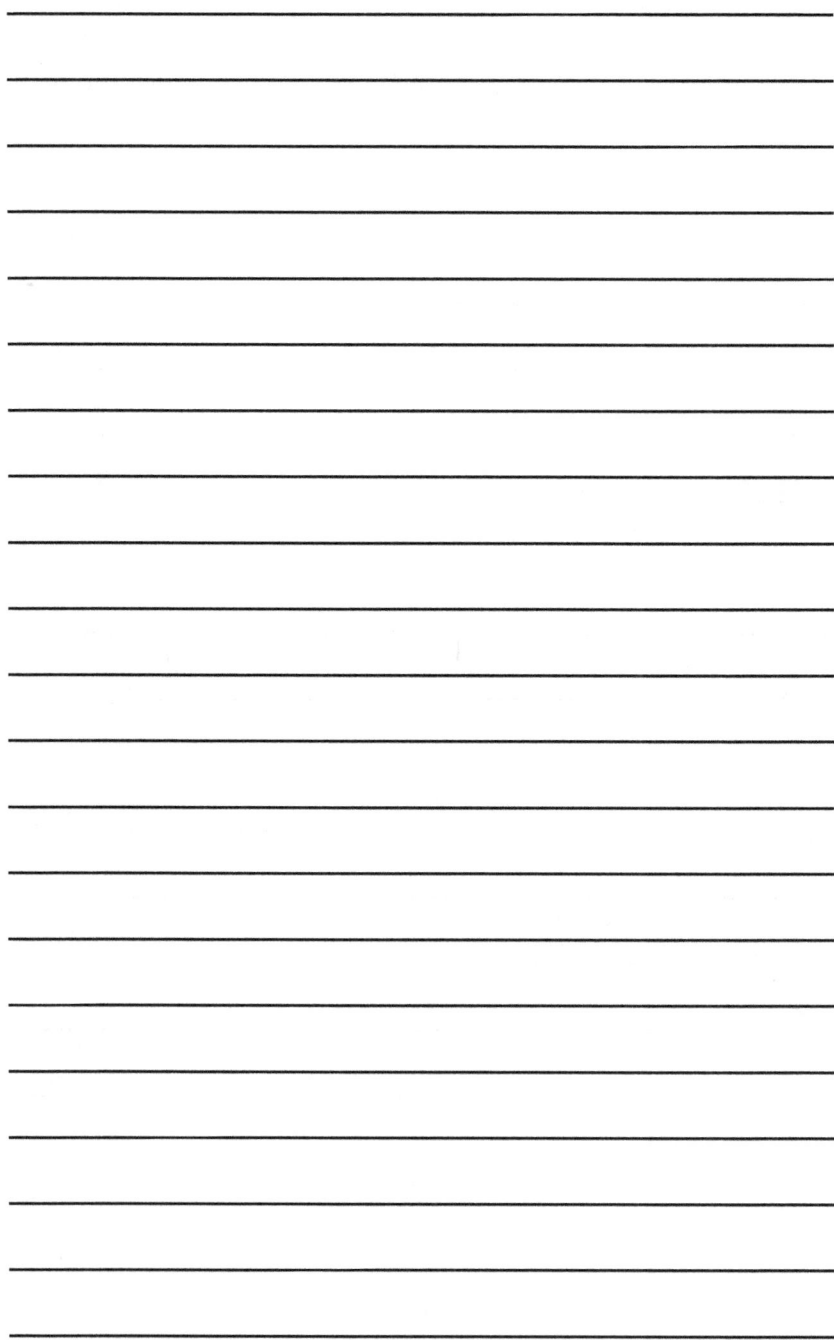

What fulfillment do you get from doing what you are passionate about?

_____

_____

_____

_____

_____

_____

_____

_____

_____

_____

_____

_____

_____

_____

_____

If you were instructed to quit fulfilling your passion, how would it make you feel?

_____

_____

_____

_____

_____

_____

_____

_____

_____

_____

_____

_____

_____

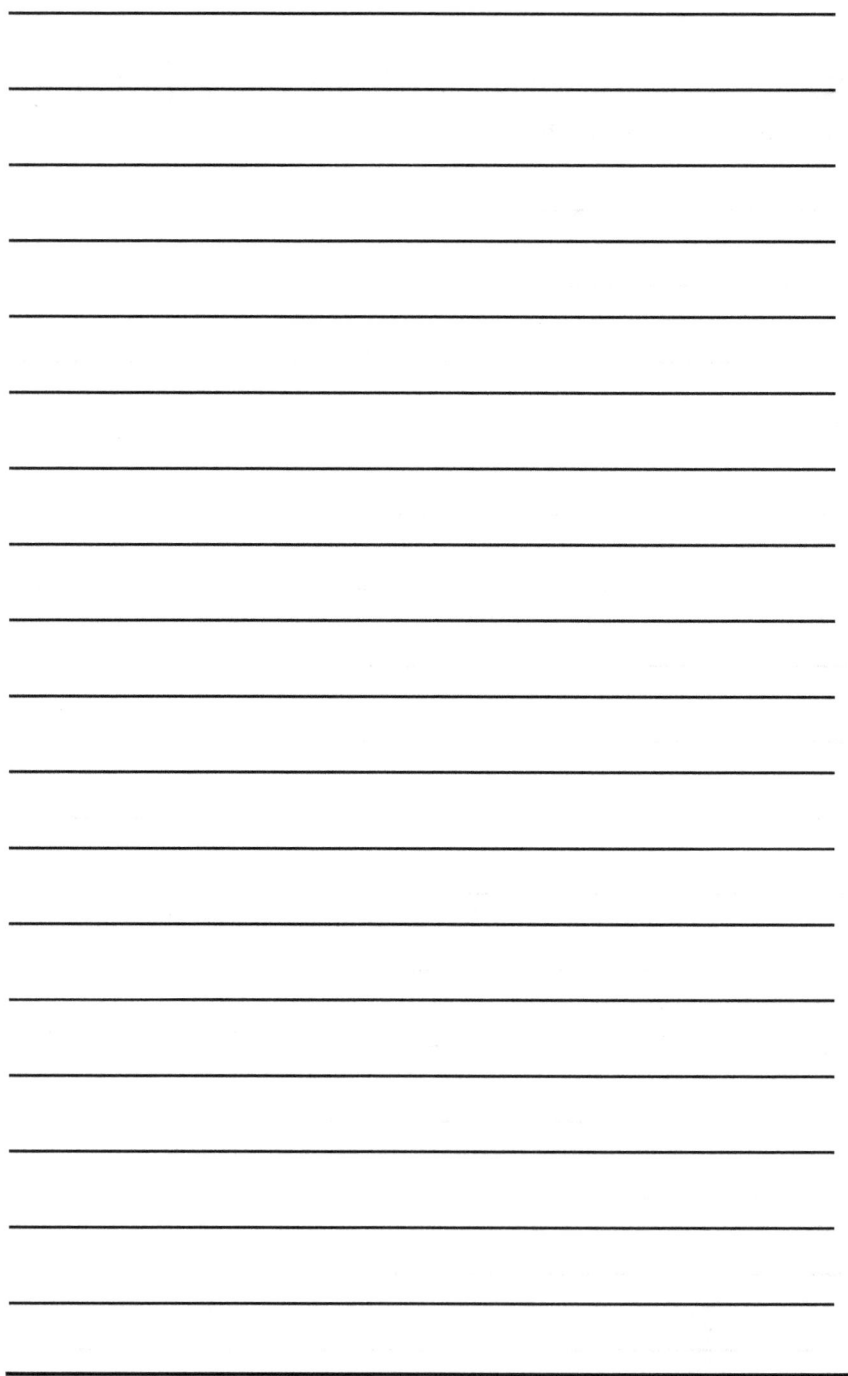

When you find your 'Why', you will be filled with mixed emotions. But ultimately, finding your 'Why' will give you a sense of pride and excitement. It's okay to be fearful (for a moment). But you have to be able to press through negative thoughts and focus on what you are passionate about.

What you are passionate about tells a lot about who you are. It is imperative to take time to discover who you are and find your 'why'. Life is short. It is time to find what motivates you in hopes of being unstoppable.

Fear vs. Failure

Fear may be described as an unpleasant emotion, while failure can be identified as simply not having success.

   Though the two words are very different, they often go hand and hand, as unpleasant emotions arise when we don't succeed.

   We are scared to fail. Therefore, we allow fear to set in not realizing that sometimes you have to fall in order to appreciate getting back up.

Name a time when you failed in life? Did failure turn to fear?

_____

_____

_____

_____

_____

_____

_____

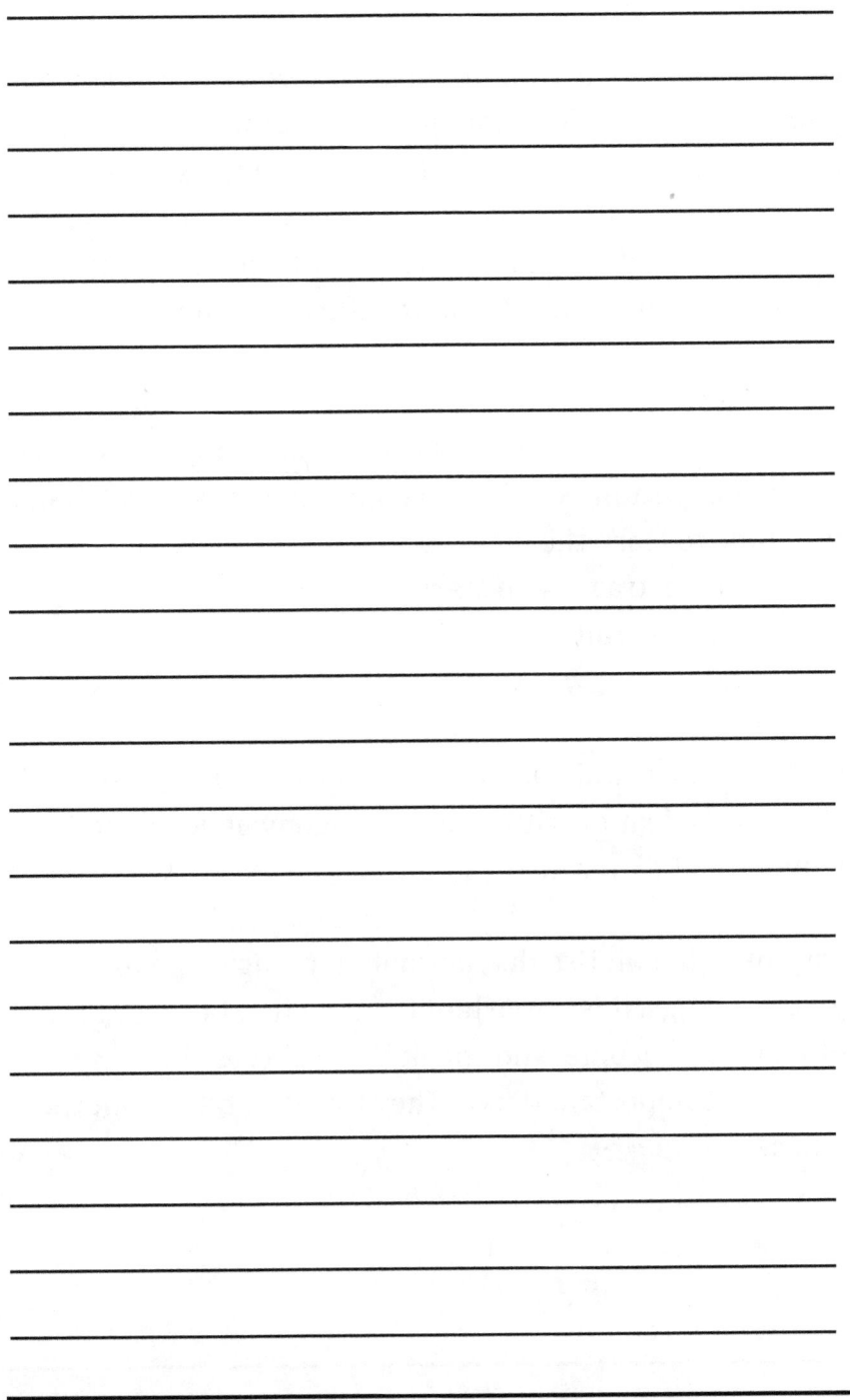

When we experience failure in life, as we all will at some point, we must understand that it is not the end. It is in those times that we must find our muse and use it as a source of guidance for when we are ready to try again. If we don't encourage ourselves and find inner strength, fear will settle in and it will be more difficult to move forward.

The first time I began writing, I failed. I didn't fail at writing. But I failed at not fully understanding that it takes more than putting words on a paper to be a writer. I didn't take time to learn the process. In the end, it cost me money and extra time to start over and work on perfecting my craft.

I often sit back and imagine where I would be now if I had allowed the fear of criticism or the agony of defeat and failure to take over me.

It's okay to fail! Use that as your stepping stone to greater things. It is important to know that because far too often we see people who speak about success but they forget one important detail. They forget to talk about the journey.

Talk about your journey. Embrace those times that you failed. It is not about how many times you fall that is important. Instead, all that counts is that you get back up. Get up and keep pressing toward your mark. Get up and look fear in the face and allow your faith to take you places beyond your greatest imagination.

The fact that you are reading this right now, at this very moment despite of all that you have endured is an accomplishment. Why? Because it proves that you are determined to be unstoppable.

No More Excuses

I was going to journal my thoughts but……

I was invited to enter a competition to promote my business but……

I want to go to the gym today but……

I am going to focus and start my own business but……

Excuses, excuses, excuses. We all have them and quite frankly I am over excuses. An excuse is your justification for why you didn't do what you needed to do in the first place.

What excuses have you made lately?

_____

Why are you constantly making excuses?

_____

_____

_____

_____

_____

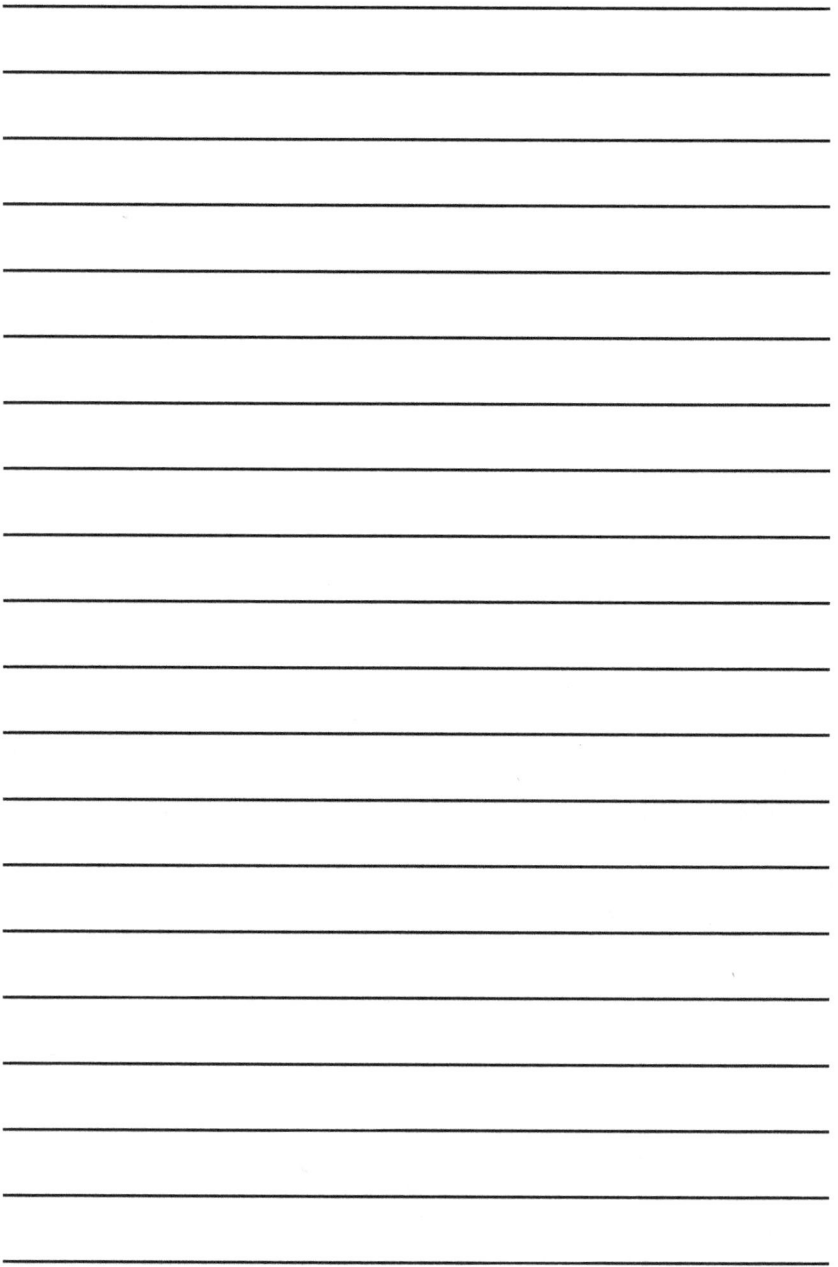

Do you know who benefits from excuses? NO ONE. Absolutely no one benefits from an excuse. It is time to slowly yet steadily stop making excuses. Every time you feel yourself making an excuse, pause and ask yourself, "How will making this excuse be beneficial to me?"

You can't be unstoppable if you are constantly stopping and make excuses. You have to make a conscious decision to remain focused. Is it okay to take a break? Of course, we all need to free our minds and mentally relax ourselves. I challenge you to stop taking the easy way out. Start setting goals and reach them. Don't let anything or anyone discourage you from being unstoppable.

_____

_____

_____

_____

_____

_____

_____

_____

_____

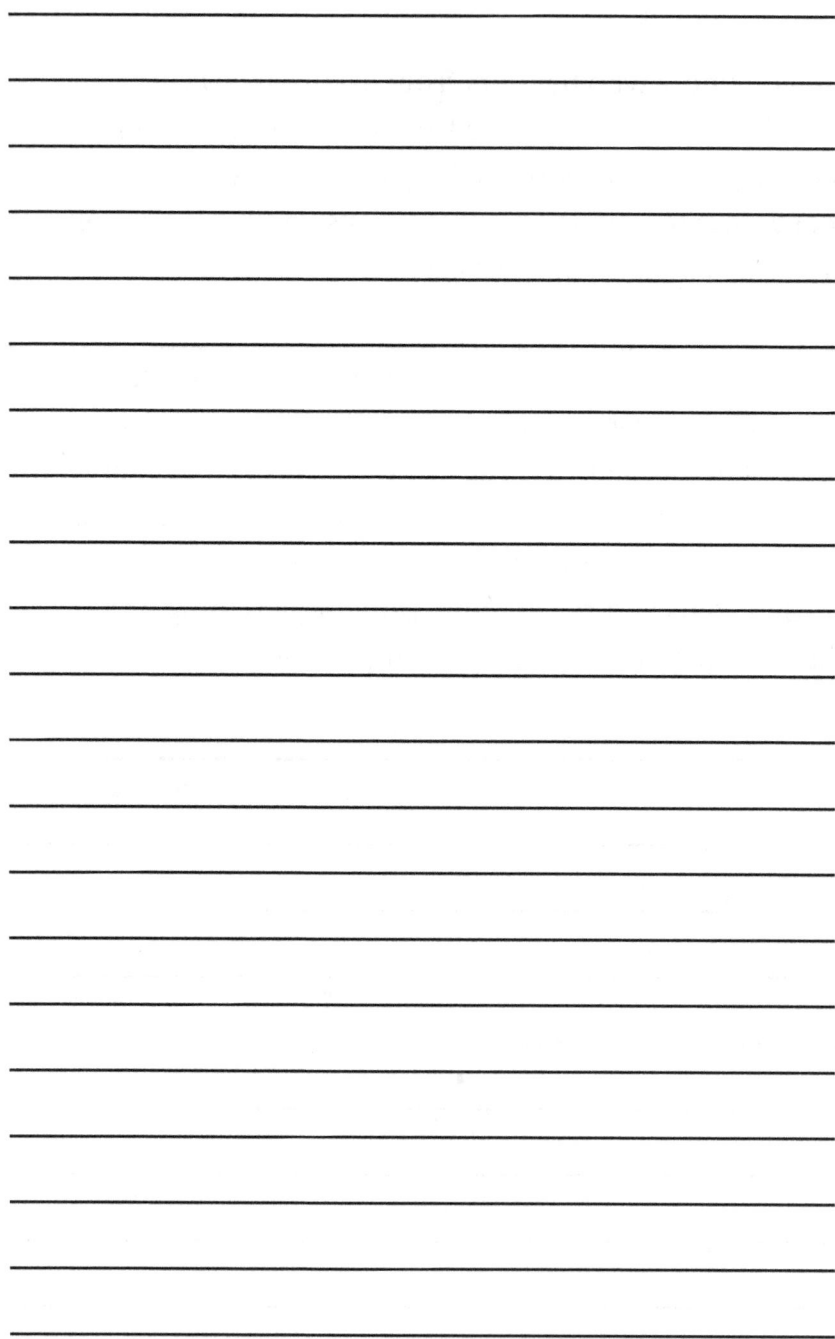

" *Today I made one choice that changed my life; I made the choice to succeed.*"

— *Lynette Edwards*

Ready, Set, Succeed

The runners are on the track. They have all undergone months of training. Each runner is determined to win the race. The announcer steps to the podium and begins to say, "On your mark, get set, go." The runners simultaneously begin to run.
Each runner looks straight ahead. Though there are multiple runners on the track, they each know that there can only be one winner.

After running the full track, one runner emerges as the winner. The runner has won the race and the race is now over. The winner of the race takes a deep breath and walks to the podium to accept the award. The winner has emerged and the race is officially over!

Track running, like other sports, has only one winner. Though many participate, only one person is the winner. The other competitors are considered losers and if they want to win, they have to go back to the drawing board, re-evaluate, retrain, and compete again in the future.

Lucky for you, your life is not set up as a competition. You are not running against anyone. You are simply your own competition. Regardless of if you choose to accomplish anything in this life or not, the choice is up to you. No one can dictate what you do or how far you make it. Only you!

Sure, money may be a factor and you may feel as though life has already passed you by. But the truth remains that as long as there is breath in your body, you still have a chance to succeed.

_____

_____

_____

_____

_____

_____

_____

_____

_____

_____

_____

_____

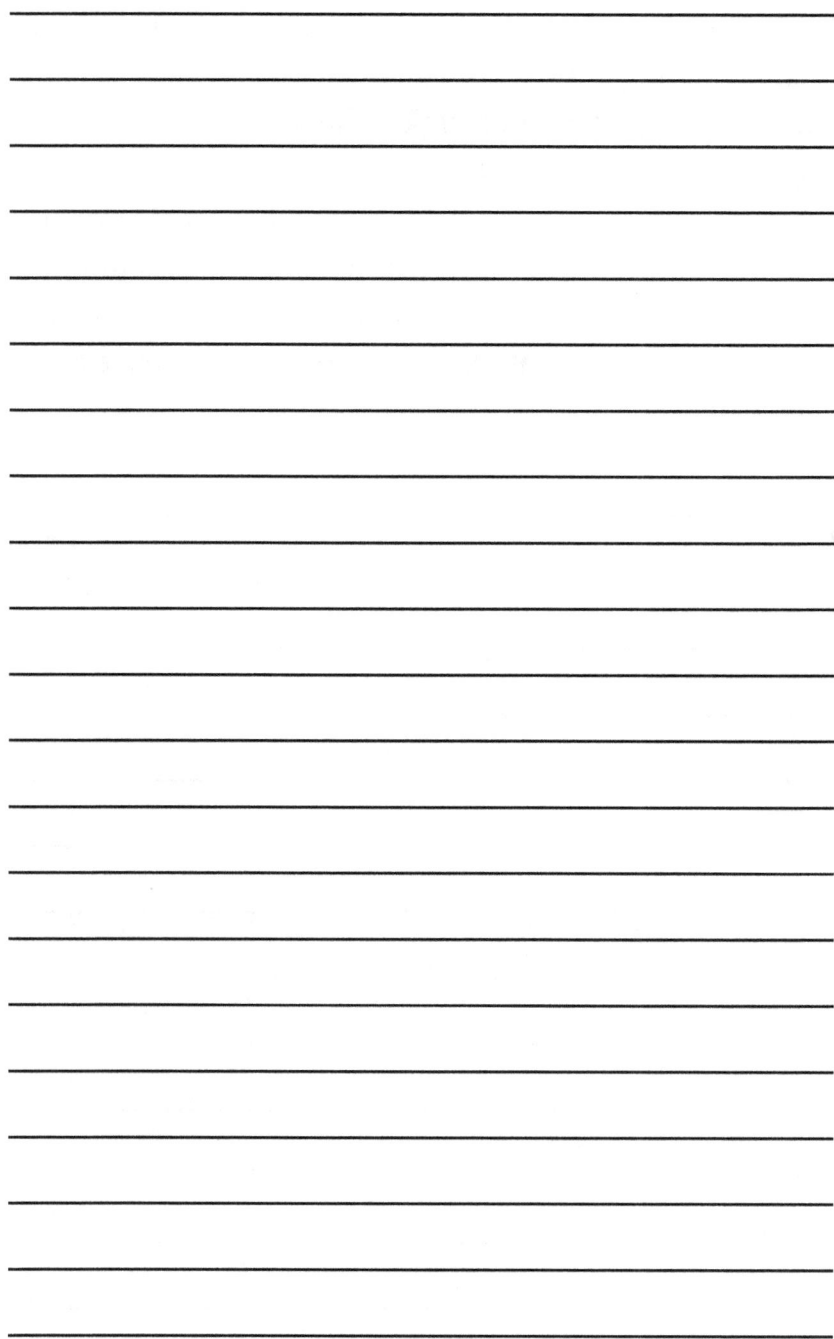

What current roadblocks are stopping you from succeeding?

_____

_____

_____

_____

_____

_____

_____

_____

_____

_____

_____

_____

_____

_____

_____

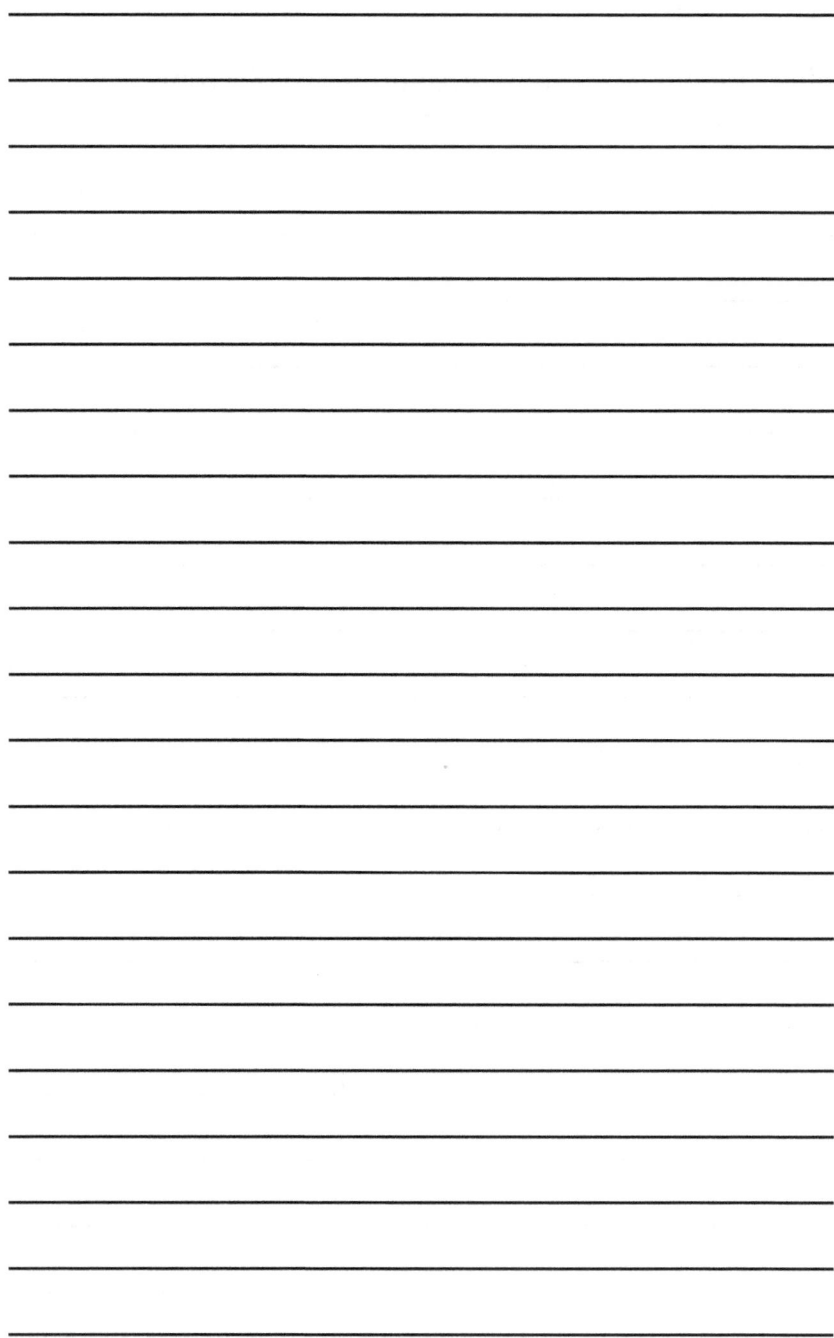

Now that you have identified roadblocks, what action steps can you take to remove all roadblocks?

_____

_____

_____

_____

_____

_____

_____

_____

_____

_____

_____

_____

_____

_____

_____

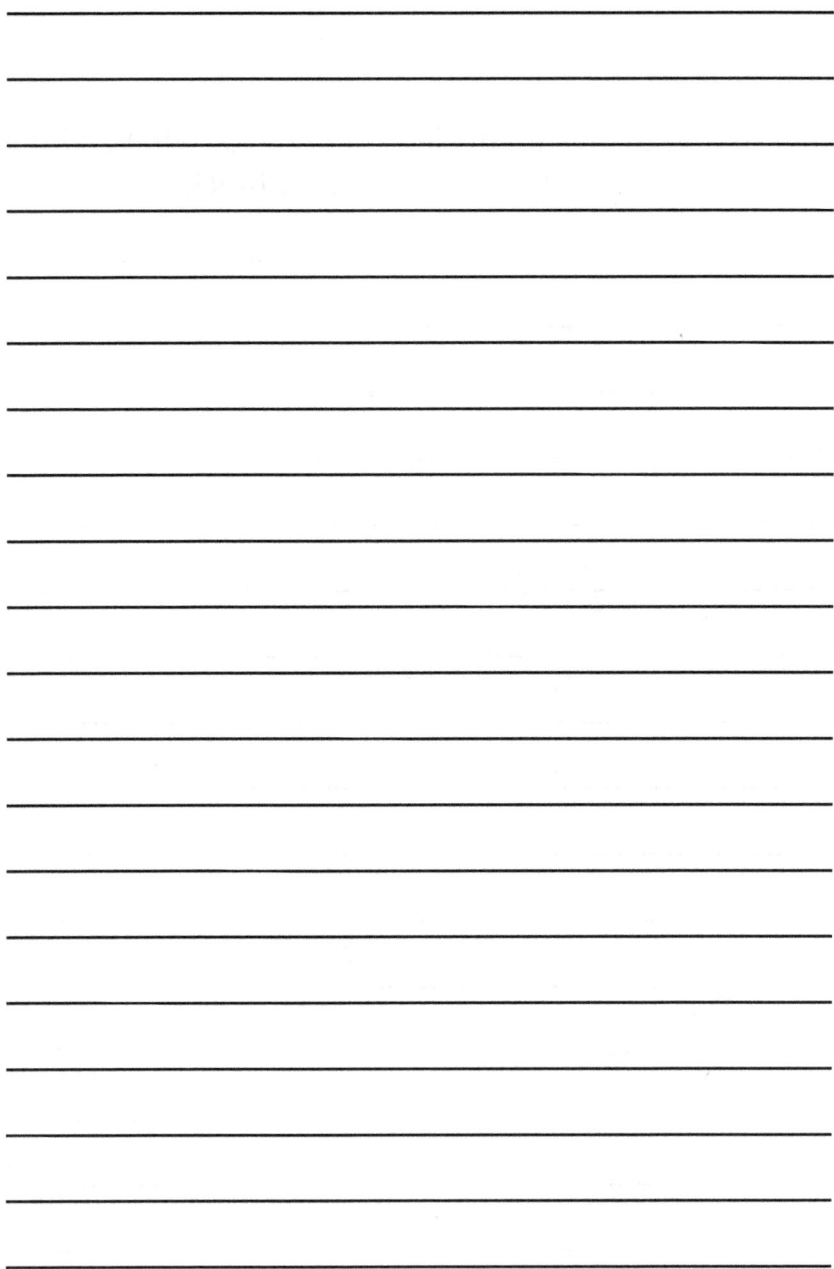

The time to succeed is now. Yesterday is gone and tomorrow is not promised. You can succeed in every area in your life, not because you have to, but simply because you can. You were born to win. You hold the keys to your future. Don't let anything or anyone hinder your success. Are you ready? It's time to go. Ready, set, succeed and be Unstoppable!

- Lynette Edwards

Be U-N-S-T-O-P-P-A-B-L-E

Circle the one word that describes how you feel at this very moment.....

Excited   Valued   Determined

Energized   Motivated   Empowered

What can you do to allow this current feeling to last a lifetime?

_____

_____

_____

_____

_____

_____

_____

_____

_____

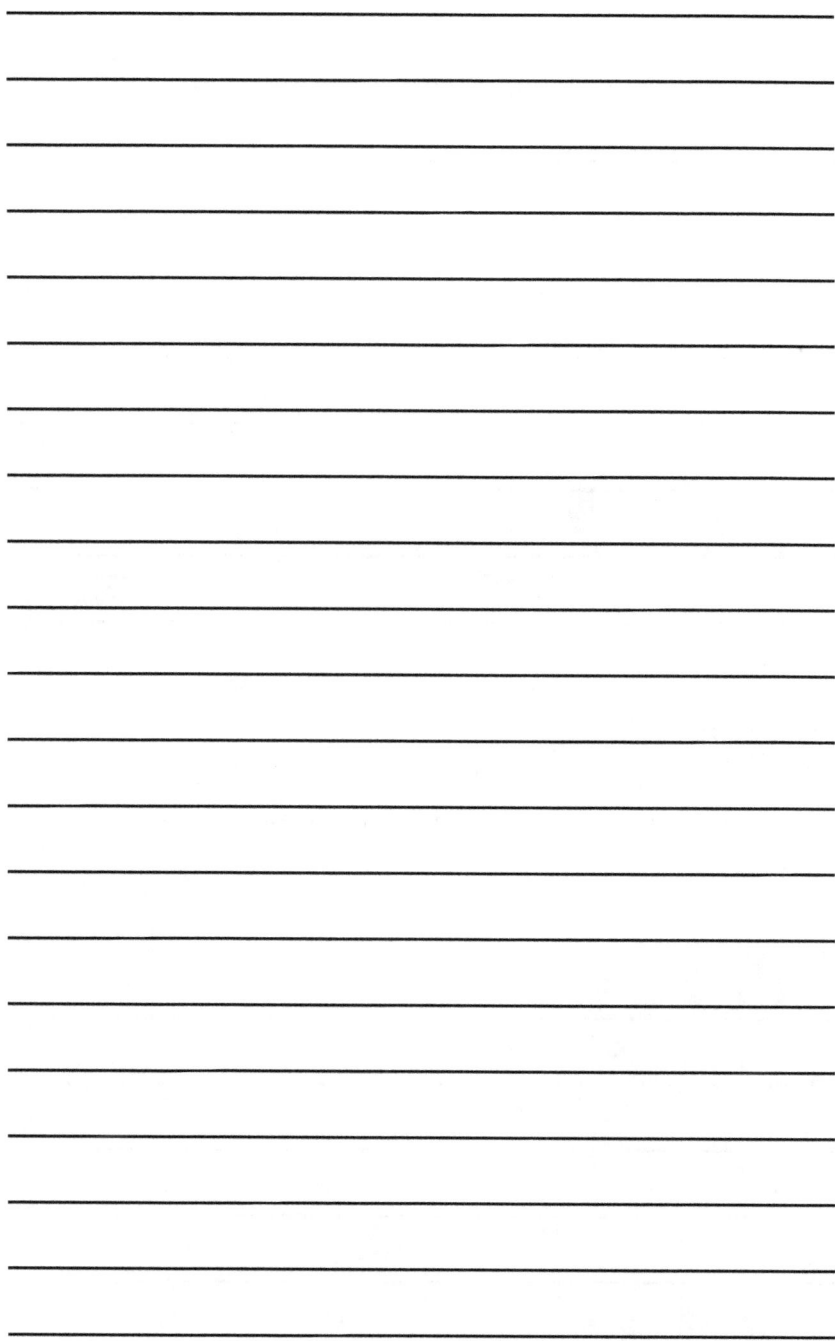

Have you learned to embrace adversity?

_____

_____

_____

_____

_____

_____

_____

_____

_____

_____

_____

_____

_____

_____

_____

_____

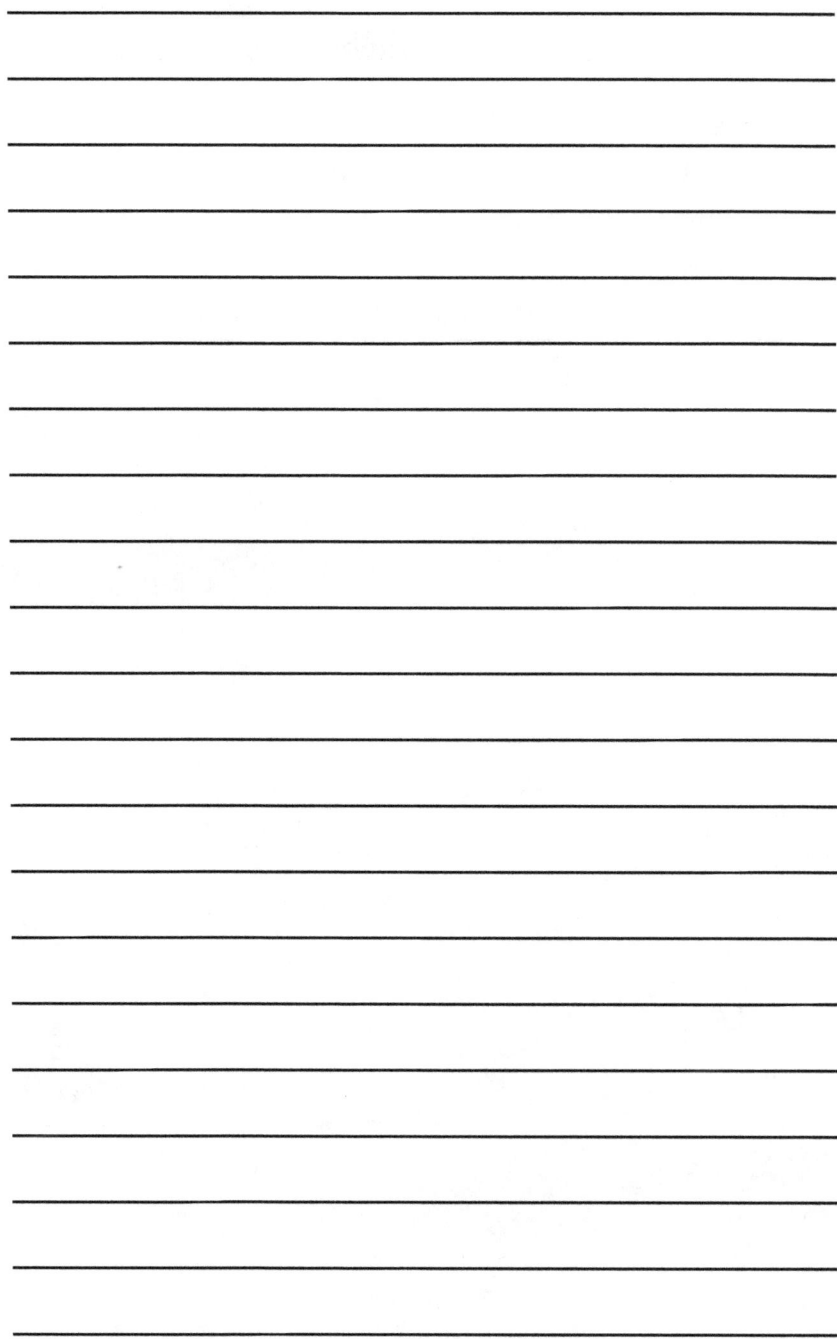

Positive ways to handle adversity on your journey:

1. Listen to soft music.
2. Light a candle and dim the lights.
3. Google your favorite scripture.
4. Look in the mirror and encourage yourself.
5. Reflect on past memories that once made you smile.

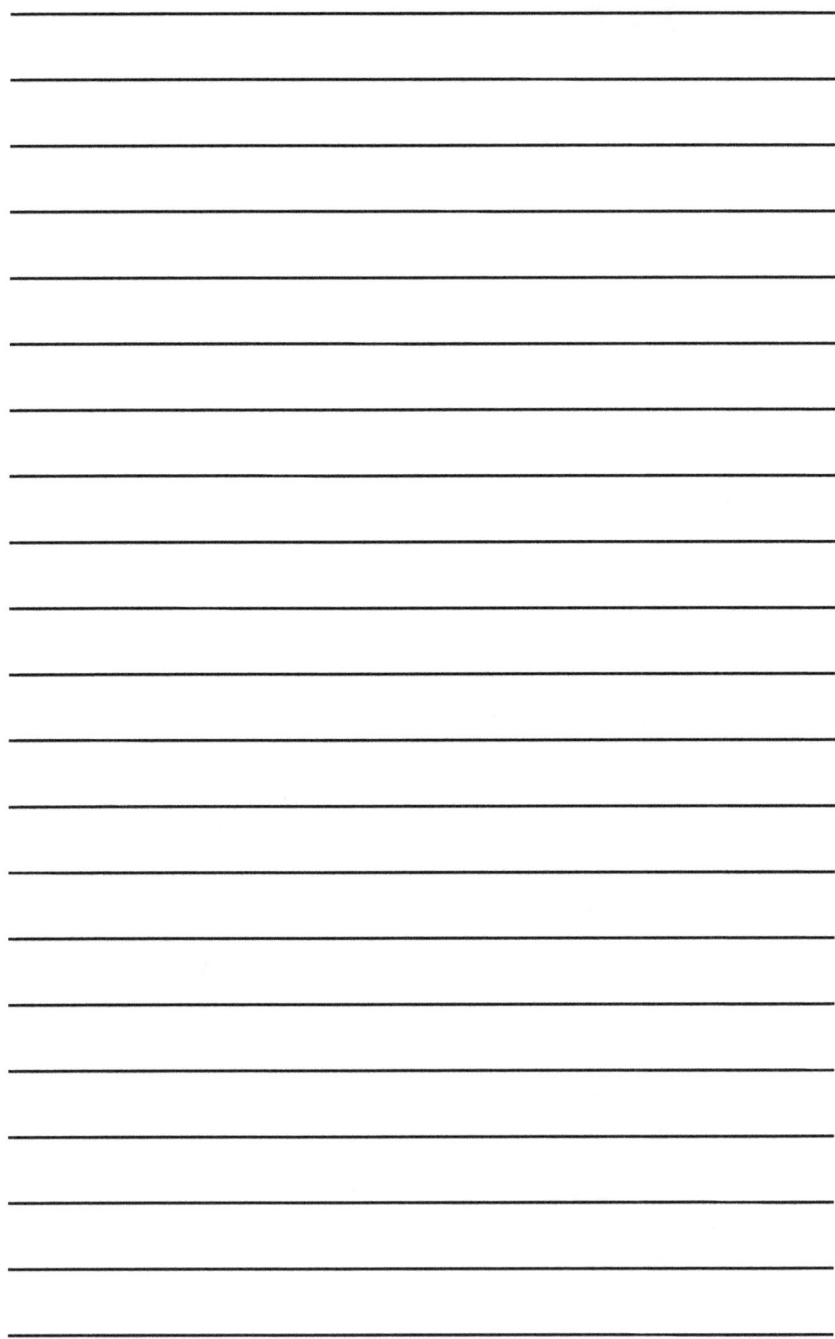

We are all different and handle life's obstacles in a variety of ways. You have to find what brings you happiness in times of adversity. It is important that you are able to reflect throughout your journey. It is equally important to know that you are unique. No two persons are alike; you are in a class by yourself, there is no competition.

- *Lynette Edwards*

What is it about you that stands out above everyone else?

_____

_____

_____

_____

_____

_____

_____

_____

_____

_____

_____

_____

_____

_____

_____

_____

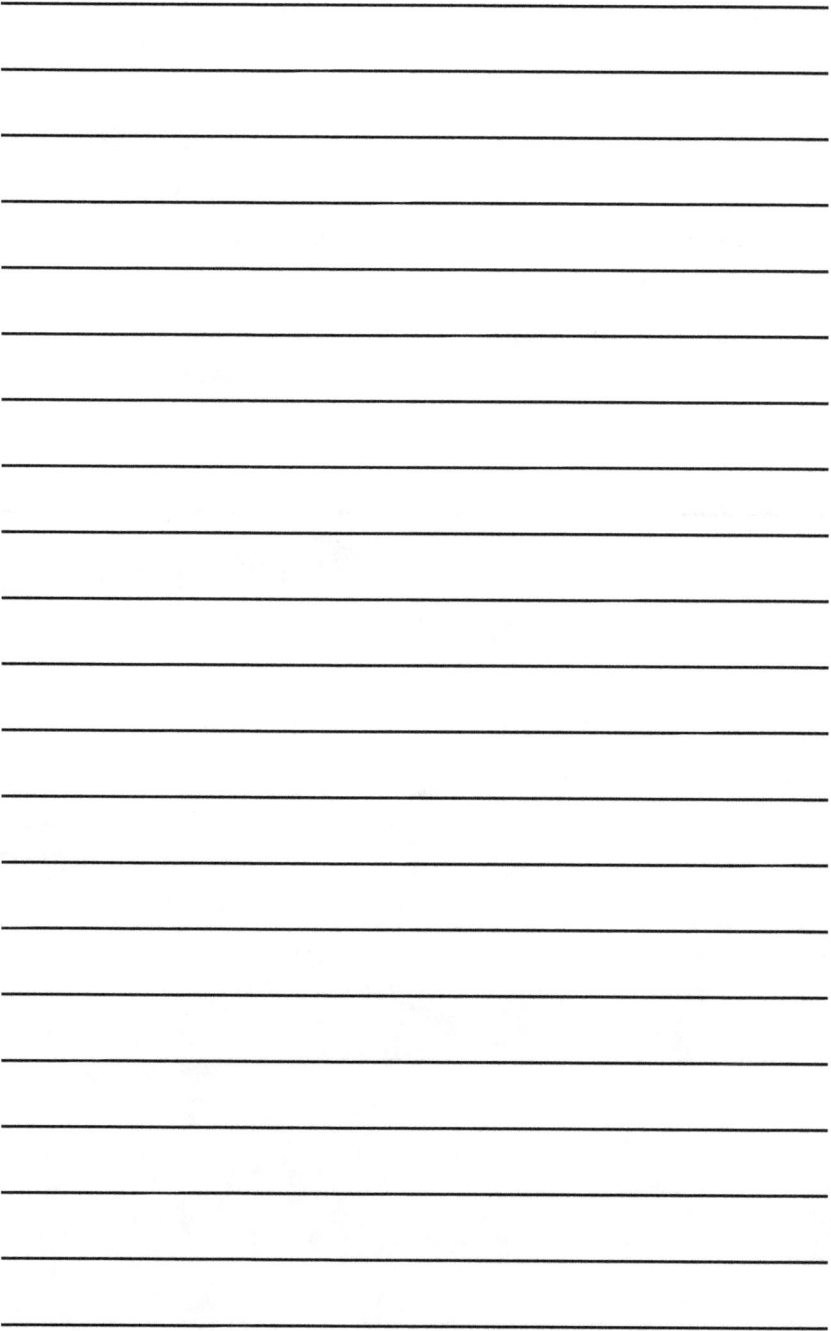

There is value in self-worth. You are priceless and you have everything you need to make it to the next level in your life. I challenge you to put yourself first. It is important to know what you bring to the table so that you don't allow anyone to undervalue who you are as a person.

_____

_____

_____

_____

_____

_____

_____

_____

_____

_____

_____

_____

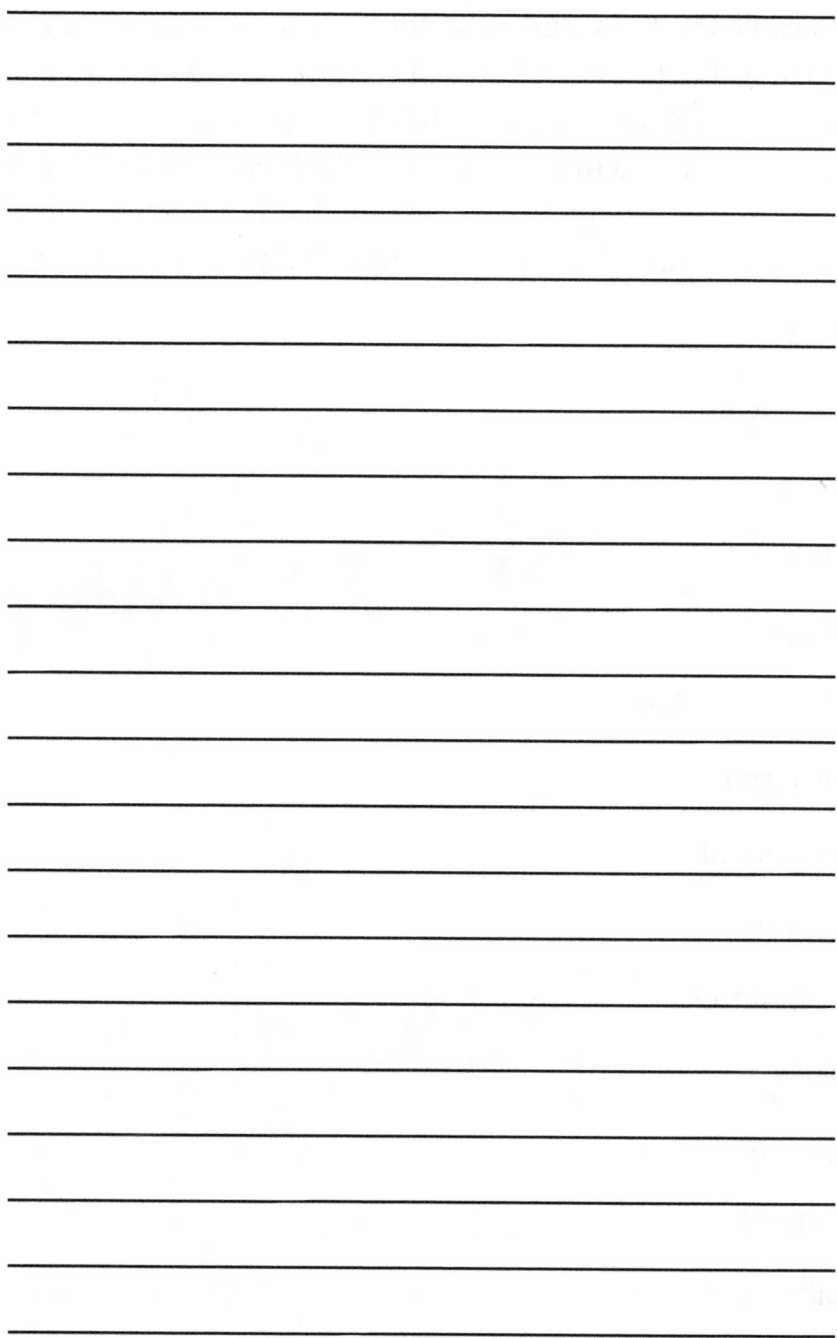

There comes a time in your life when you must give up the 'I can't' for 'I can' and move forward on your journey. The road will not be easy. You will endure some dark days and encounter many sleepless nights. But you cannot quit. It is during those times that you should remember why you started. Reignite that passion that is already instilled inside of you and make a conscious decision to keep going.

I AM......

Empowered

Bold

Unique

Fearless

Understanding

Inspired

Persistent

Driven

Committed

Wise

Qualified

Powerful

Liberated

Authentic

I AM U-N-S-T-O-P-P-A-B-L-E

_____

_____

_____

_____

_____

_____

_____

_____

_____

_____

_____

_____

_____

_____

_____

_____

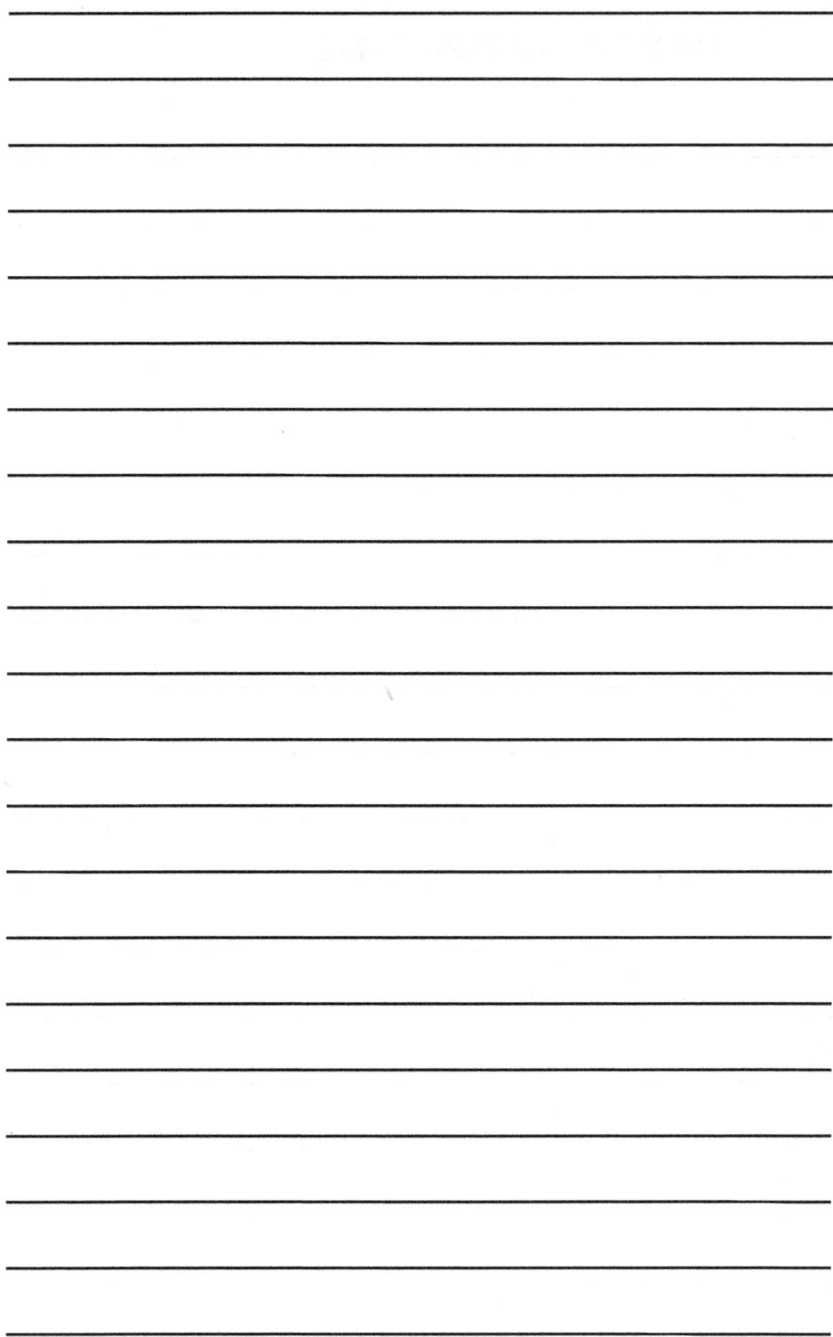

You have freed your mind, released negativity, and set goals. You are now determined. You understand your wants versus your needs. You are able to embrace rejection and most of all, you are aware of the power of self-investment. You are a Goal-Getter who knows the importance of daily reflection. You are motivated because you discovered your 'WHY'. Fear and failure are no longer options because there are no more excuses! You are ready to succeed. In fact, you are officially UNSTOPPABLE!

- Lynette Edwards

Get To Know The Writer.....

Lynette Edwards began her writing career in 2011, when she was given a book filled with inspiring women by a family member. Lynette briefly looked through the pages of the book. But instead of reading the book, she decided to write her own story.

While writing Lynette found peace of mind, she soon discovered that writing allowed her to release emotions that she was not able to verbalize. She began traveling to different states, touring, conducting radio interviews, premiering on national television, and taking her books to new levels. In 2016 she served as the Executive Producer of the theatrical performance *One Night Only*. The production was inspired by one of her books.

In addition, Lynette has been honored with writing awards, plaques, and has served on various panels as a featured author. Lynette hopes to continue to inspire others and leave an impact through her written words.

Lynette believes that everything in life is a lesson or a blessing and she firmly believes that the best is yet to come.

Books by Lynette Edwards:

Just a Little Talk with Jesus

Take off the Mask

Uncompromising Love

Still Standing

One Night Only

We Have Only Just Begun

Playing with Fire

In addition to being a published author, Lynette is also a Life Coach.

www.AuthorLynette.com

I am UNSTOPPABLE because.....

_____

_____

_____

_____

_____

_____

_____

_____

_____

_____

_____

_____

_____

_____

_____

_____

I am UNSTOPPABLE because.....

_____

_____

_____

_____

_____

_____

_____

_____

_____

_____

_____

_____

_____

_____

_____

_____

_____

_____

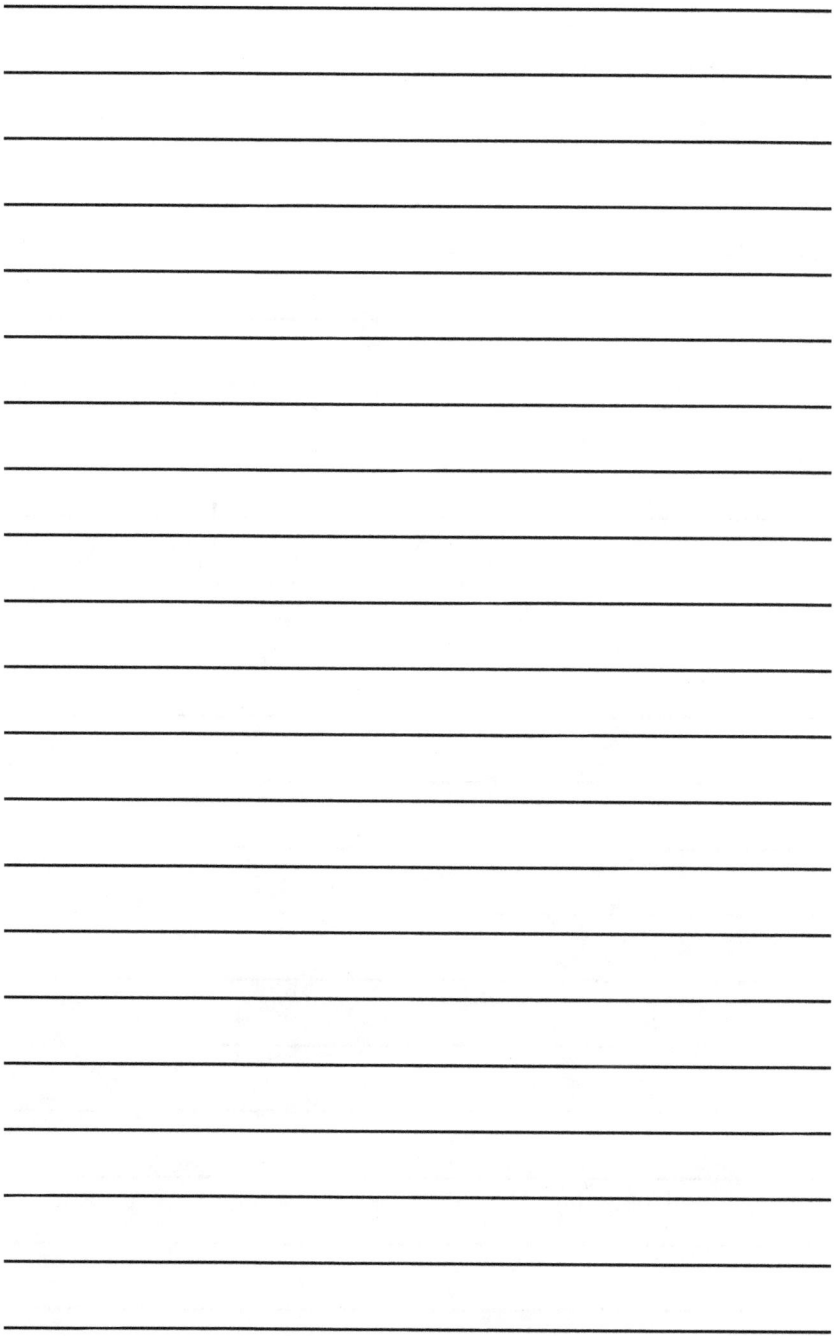

I am UNSTOPPABLE because.....

_____

_____

_____

_____

_____

_____

_____

_____

_____

_____

_____

_____

_____

_____

_____

_____

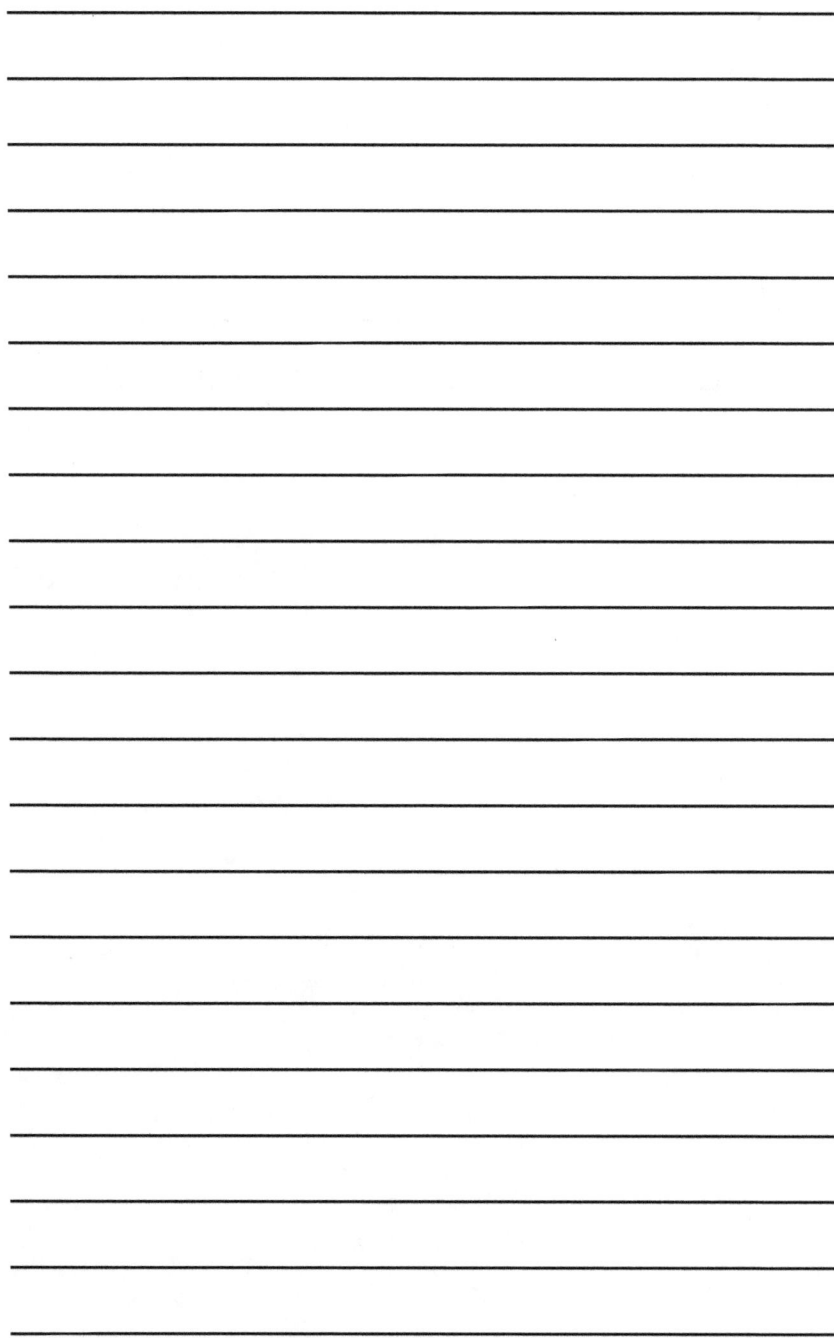

My name is _____
and I am…….Unstoppable.

www.ingramcontent.com/pod-product-compliance
Lightning Source LLC
Chambersburg PA
CBHW071221090426
42736CB00014B/2925